A NEW ZEALAND

Country Harvest

COOKBOOK

Delicious traditional and new
recipes for jams, preserves,
chutneys, pickles and baking.

GILIAN PAINTER

A NEW ZEALAND

Country Harvest

COOKBOOK

Delicious traditional and new recipes for jams, preserves, chutneys, pickles and baking.

GILIAN PAINTER

Contents

VIKING

Penguin Books (NZ) Ltd, cnr Rosedale and Airborne Roads, Albany, Auckland, New Zealand
Penguin Books Ltd, 27 Wrights Lane, London W8 5TZ, England
Penguin USA, 375 Hudson Street, New York, NY 10014, United States
Penguin Books Australia Ltd, 487 Maroondah Highway, Ringwood, Australia 3134
Penguin Books Canada Ltd, 10 Alcorn Avenue, Toronto, Ontario, Canada M4V 3B2

Penguin Books Ltd, Registered Offices: Harmondsworth, Middlesex, England

First published by Penguin Books (NZ) Ltd 1997
1 3 5 7 9 10 8 6 4 2

Cover design by V8
Printed in Hong Kong
ISBN 0 670 87837 5

Weight and Temperature Conversion Guide

While not exact, the following conversions are convenient compromises which will work with the recipes in this book.

5 cm   =   2 inches

50 g   =   2 oz

125 g   =   4 oz

250 g   =   8 oz / $\frac{1}{2}$ lb

500 g   =   1 lb

1 kg   =   2 lbs

1 litre   =   2 pints

Degrees Celsius	Degrees Fahrenheit	Gas
110-140	225-275	$\frac{1}{4}$-1
150-160	300-325	2-3
180-190	350-375	4-5
200-230	400-450	6-8

And all thy cloisters smell of apple orchards,
And there are lilies white and small red roses
And every bird sings in the early morning
Lament for Alcuin.
Anon. 9th century

Acknowledgements

Men and women have been exchanging recipes since time and cooking began, and a study of early cookery books shows how recipes have changed and developed according to the ingredients and cooking equipment available. Our pioneering ancestors brought with them their favourite plants and trees and established gardens and orchards in the southern hemisphere after the pattern of those at 'Home'.

They brought their recipes, too, gradually adapting them to different climates and seasons. Their handwritten recipe books record not only the ingredients and methods but often the names of family and friends who shared the recipes — 'Aunt Nellie's Plum Pudding', 'Alice's Chocolate Cake' and the like.

My grandmother's own book included knitting patterns and some Victorian puzzles and games. We also have the great scrapbook of pictures made especially to entertain her children on the long sea voyage from England when she and my grandfather emigrated to Australia, then New Zealand, in the 1870s.

My grandmother did not survive long in the new land, dying just a month after my father was born. My great-grandmother took over the household for some years until grandfather married again. Because of this early influence, many of the recipes my father enjoyed were really those of the mid-nineteenth century and even earlier, related more to the cooking of Hannah Glasse than Isabella Beeton.

My mother's great-grandfather came to South Australia in 1840 from Ireland with his 'Dear Wife Mary and five children'. My mother was of the second generation of her family to be born in Australia.

When I grew up, there were both Australian and New Zealand recipe books in the kitchen drawer and when I came to compile *this* book, I found myself unable to really separate the two geographical/cultural influences. I have to acknowledge with gratitude the long line of cooks on both sides of my family who have handed down their recipes to me.

I have received many recipes from friends, too — Diana Allan, Horace Carrington, Jean Dickson, Gertrude Foster, Jan Jones, Lesley van Alphen and Jeanette Zudmeer. The recipes of Mrs Brocket, mother of my friend Anne Simpson, and Mrs Carlyle, mother of my friend Jeanne Russell, are also gratefully acknowledged.

Thanks, too, to my friend Tui Flower who willingly shares her professional knowledge and sound advice; to Stephen Barnett for his patient editing; to Julie McNally who did much of the cooking used in the pictures, and to Norman Zammit, without whose beautiful photography this book would be only words!

As always, I must acknowledge the help and support of my loving husband, Philip.

Introduction

In the far-off leisurely days of my childhood, harvesting was a way of life. There was the daily harvest for the table of flowers, fruit and vegetables and the seasonal harvest for the store cupboards — jams, chutneys, pickles and bottled fruit. There were also special harvests, lavender for the linen cupboard, pine cones for the fire and autumn mushrooms for breakfast. Life on the edge of town was measured by the seasonal foods from the garden and the kitchen was the most important room in the house. This may all seem old-fashioned but it was a very satisfying way to live, and live well.

Home-made preserves have a flavour all of their own because they are made in small quantities and do not have to conform to standards for shelf-life. And, when the raw materials are home-grown fruit and vegetables, they can be harvested at the peak of perfection.

Bottling fruit was a summer occupation — apricots, plums, peaches, nectarines, pears and apples were cooked by the bucketful in a light syrup so that there would be plenty of summer tastes in winter. The simplest dessert was a jar of fruit served with cream; if there was time, it would be made into a crumble, pie, or sponge pudding.

I don't know which I enjoyed most, the harvesting or the cooking, but from an early age I was picking strawberries, currants and gooseberries, climbing apple trees to get the topmost fruit and fighting my way into the blackberry patch in the paddock with a billy — one blackberry for jam, one for me.

Then there were the days at the kitchen table stoning peaches or slicing grapefruit for marmalade. There were interesting gadgets like a dual bean slicer, which would cut up two scarlet runners at a time, and my mother's great wooden spoon that allowed us to stir the jam on the coal range without getting too hot.

Certain crops like gherkins were especially grown for pickling but most of the produce from the garden was eaten fresh in season, with excess exchanged with the neighbours or made into jams, pickles or chutneys.

As each new thing came into season, it would be cooked and served with modest celebration — the first asparagus (with melted butter), green peas (with mint), or strawberries (with sugar and cream). The garden was large with about 15 fruit trees and a number of vegetable beds including a strawberry bed, an asparagus bed and a large patch

'The front garden was for flowers . . .'

of Jerusalem artichokes. There were also two hen-houses so we always had fresh eggs, and poultry for high days and holidays.

The front garden was for flowers — Iceland poppies, anemones and ranunculus in spring with freesias, grape hyacinths and daffodils. Dahlias and beautiful hydrangeas in summer and, in autumn, chrysanthemums and — later — berries, camellias and violets — my favourite.

My parents enjoyed their garden and worked in it most days, depending on the weather. They were aware of the seasons and the stars, sun, rain and frost. They worked hard but still had time to watch a bee in a flower, listen to the birds and spend time with their friends.

It may be that I look back with nostalgia but I also look forward with confidence for I feel sure that, in spite of the apparent takeover of technology, many people still find happiness and fulfilment living more quietly in country surroundings, growing and harvesting good food in the age-old pattern of the seasons.

GILIAN PAINTER

Jams, Jellies, Marmalades, Curds
& OTHER SWEET TREATS

The equipment listed below is used to make jams, jellies and marmalades.

1. A preserving pan or large saucepan big enough to contain fruit and its juice or water and the necessary quantity of sugar, big enough to allow the contents to come to a rolling boil without overflowing.

2. A wooden spoon for stirring the jam or jelly (a metal spoon quickly becomes too hot to hold).

3. A slotted spoon to scoop out stones as they rise to the surface of the jam.

4. A sieve for straining out pips or stones while allowing pulp to pass through and back into the jam pan.

5. A jelly bag or large piece of fine cloth through which the juice can be strained, leaving the pulp in the bag.

6. A small bag or piece of fine cloth in which to tie pips and peels to add to jam or marmalade to provide extra pectin while the jam is cooking, though this should be removed before the sugar is added.

7. A plastic or pyrex jug for pouring jam or jelly safely from the preserving pan into heated jars.

8. Scales to weigh fruit and sugar accurately.

9. Jars of a size suitable to your needs, with lids or cellophane covers.

10. A sharp knife for preparing fruit.

11. A rubber spatula for cleaning all the jam out of the pan and jug.

12. A lemon squeezer and a lemon zester.

13. An apron to protect clothing from fruit splatters which result in hard-to-remove stains.

JAMS

Jam, according to *The Oxford English Dictionary*, is 'a conserve of fruit made by boiling it with sugar to a thick consistency.'

The fruit should be ripe but not overripe because then it lacks enough acid and pectin to set satisfactorily. The fruit should be picked when dry (after the dew has evaporated and not on a wet day), and any blemishes or bird specks should be cut out with a sharp knife and discarded. Fruit with any mould or brown rot should not be used. Some fruits such as strawberries, figs, peaches and pears do not contain enough acid and pectin to set, so are often combined with apple, lemon juice or other acid fruits such as redcurrants or gooseberries. I add lemon juice to most jams as a matter of course and rarely experience problems with setting. The other essential ingredient is sugar. This may be white or an unrefined demerara or raw sugar, but not brown sugar as it is too moist and 'treacly' to use in jam making.

Do not make large quantities of jam — no more than 2 kg of fruit at a time gives best results.

Weigh and prepare the fruit according to the recipe. If the fruit is to be left unpeeled, like plums, butter the bottom of the jam pan lightly to stop the skins sticking. Put the fruit in the pan, with or without liquid, and bring it to the boil, stirring it evenly with the wooden spoon. Lower the heat and cook the fruit gently until it is soft. Then gradually add the sugar, stirring until it is completely dissolved before raising the heat and bringing the jam to a rolling boil. Boil until it sets when tested on a saucer. Continue to stir now and then and watch it well because it can easily boil over, or burn if the heat is too high, and cleaning sticky jam off the top of the stove is just about as bad as cleaning the oven!

Testing for setting

Because every batch of fruit is different it is impossible in most cases to give an exact boiling time to set the jam. However, as you stir you will notice that as setting approaches, the jam will begin to feel thick around the edge of the pan, and if you lift the spoon up the jam no longer runs off it but drops more slowly. At this stage take out about a teaspoon of jam and put it on a saucer. Leave it a few minutes at room temperature and then tilt the saucer. If the jam wrinkles it is ready, if it just runs it is not. Lower the heat or remove the pan from the heat while you test the jam so it does not overcook. If it will set, turn the heat off. If there is any white froth on top of the jam, drop a teaspoon of butter into the middle of the pan. This will cause the pectin froth to move to the side of the pan where it can be skimmed off with a metal spoon and discarded.

Fill the jam jars with hot water in the sink and when they are heated through tip the water into a basin and dry the jars thoroughly. Fill each with jam to about 1 cm from the rim using a plastic jug. Stand the hot jars on a wooden board or a folded newspaper — not a cold bench — to prevent them cracking. Completely clean out the pan and the jug with the rubber spatula but do not add any of the thick pectin froth to the jam. Tip the hot water out of the basin into the pan, top it up with more water if necessary and clean all the jam-making equipment straight away. Wipe any spills off the side of the jars and the bench. If you are using vacuum seal lids screw them on straight away. Otherwise allow the jam to cool completely before covering, to prevent condensation which may cause the top of the jam to go mouldy.

Cellophane jam covers, dampened one side with a wet cloth and fastened, damp-side-out, with a rubber band are quite satisfactory for jams that are set firmly. If the jam sets only softly it will not keep so well and a layer of paraffin wax which excludes the air will improve the keeping quality. To use paraffin wax cut some off the block into a clean tin, stand this in a saucepan of hot water and bring the water to the boil to melt the wax. *Never* heat the wax in a saucepan directly on the stove because it easily catches fire. When the wax melts hold the tin carefully with a folded cloth and pour a thin layer of wax over the *cold* jam to seal the jar all the way round. Then cover with cellophane. When you come to use the jam the wax will lift off cleanly. It can be washed and put back in the wax tin to be re-melted and used again.

Storing Jam

It is important to store jam and all preserves in a cool, dry place, preferably in a dark cupboard where the temperature is even. Jam is more likely to go mouldy on top if stored in a damp place. Other factors which induce mould are using wet fruit, insufficient cooking, or too little sugar being used. Mould will also develop if the jam is not properly covered. If you notice mould developing lift it off and also remove 2 cm of jam so that no mouldy flavour remains. The remainder should be all right if used quickly.

If jam is kept too long it can become sugary on top. This crust, too, can be removed and the jam used for cooking. If jam ferments it generally means that it was not properly cooked, the fruit was of poor quality or the covering of the jam not airtight which allowed yeasts into the jam. This is more likely to happen if the jam is stored in too warm a place.

Jam should not be stored in the refrigerator for any length of time because it crystallises. It is better to pot it in small jars so that it is eaten quickly rather than use large jars which take too long to finish.

All jam should be labelled with its name and the date and older jam used before beginning the new season's jam.

Jam can be made throughout the year from almost all fruit and can be used not only as a spread on toast and breads but also as a filling for cakes, biscuits and tarts, and as a sauce or topping.

Rhubarb Jam

Rhubarb is the first of the spring 'fruits' in colder climates. The plump stems are used — never the poisonous leaves — and they have a refreshing sourish flavour. The zest and juice of lemon, orange or grapefruit combines well with rhubarb and so does ginger. Try different combinations to suit your taste.

1.5 kg rhubarb
½ cup water
2 lemons or 1 orange or 1 grapefruit
25 g root ginger
1.5 kg sugar
3 tablespoons chopped crystallised ginger

String the rhubarb, cut it into 5 cm pieces and put it in a pan with ½ cup of water. Add the zest and juice of 2 lemons or the zest and pulp of an orange or a grapefruit. Bruise the root ginger and add it too. Cook gently, stirring, until the rhubarb is tender. Taste the jam and remove the root ginger when the flavour is strong enough. Add the sugar, stir well to dissolve it completely then bring the jam to a rolling boil. Add chopped crystallised ginger and continue to stir and boil the jam until setting point is reached. When it is ready stand the jam to cool slightly before potting.

Gooseberry Jam

Picking goosegogs (gooseberries) for my Dad and getting spiked on the thorny bushes is another childhood memory. He and my aunt loved gooseberries but Mum and I had reservations. Now I like them but the climate is too hot to grow them. They can be bought sometimes in the supermarket and freeze well for gooseberry fool and other puddings. Slightly underripe gooseberries are best for jam.

1.5 kg gooseberries
3 cups water
1.5 kg sugar

Top and tail the gooseberries with a sharp knife or scissors, put them in the pan with the water and bring to the boil, stirring. Cook gently until the skins are tender. (If you add the sugar too soon the skins become tough.) Add the sugar slowly, stirring to dissolve it, and bring the jam to a fast boil. Cook until it will set when tested.

Loquat and Lemon Jam

The loquat or Japanese medlar is the earliest of the tree fruit in our garden. It is an irregular cropper but I love the sweet almondy scent of the flowers and the slightly furry down on the smooth-skinned yellow fruit. Although it is the size of a large plum, most of the loquat fruit consists of large brown seeds. When just ripe they make an orange-gold-coloured jam.

2 kg stoned loquats
2½ cups water
2 lemons
2½ cups water
3 kg sugar

Cut the ends off the loquats, pop out the seeds and weigh the fruit. Put in a pan with 2½ cups of water, bring to the boil and cook until soft — this takes at least 1 hour. In another saucepan combine the sliced lemon, without any pips, and the other 2½ cups of water, simmer gently for 30 minutes and cool with the lid on. When the fruit is soft, strain the lemon water into it and stir in the sugar until dissolved. Boil fast until the jam will set when tested. A few loquat pips may be cooked in a muslin bag with the fruit to give an almondy flavour. Remove when it is to your taste. This is an adaptation of a friend's recipe.

Mulberry Jam

The birds generally get more mulberries than we do and they fall and form a fruity carpet under the tree. Black mulberries, not white (silkworm) mulberries are the better fruit but their juice stains fingers, mouths and clothes. It is a good idea to spread an old sheet on the ground under the tree to catch the berries.

1.5 kg mulberries
500 g apples
1.75 kg sugar

Place the mulberries in a pan and simmer gently in their own juice until tender. Peel, core and chop the apples and simmer separately in a small amount of water until tender. Combine the fruit and stir well. Then stir in the sugar until it dissolves and boil fast until the jam will set.

If the mulberries need washing put small quantities in a sieve, dip it in and out of a basin of cold water and drain the berries carefully. This prevents unnecessary bruising of the delicate fruit.

Strawberry Jam

Strawberry jam is very sweet — too sweet for some tastes but a favourite for others. It is a difficult jam to set and the fruit used should never be overripe. In fact just-ripe fruit makes the best jam. Jam that won't set makes a good ice-cream topping.

2 kg strawberries
juice of 1-2 lemons
2 kg sugar

Hull the strawberries and put them in the pan with the lemon juice. Heat gently, crushing the fruit with the wooden spoon to make the juice run. Simmer till soft, about 10 minutes. Add the sugar slowly, stirring to dissolve it. Bring to the boil and boil for 10 minutes only. Remove from the heat and stand 5 minutes before pouring into jars, so that the fruit is evenly distributed. Cover when cold. Because it is a soft-set jam, strawberry jam does not keep so well as some others. Overboiling makes strawberry glue!

Blueberry Jam

Blueberries are a relatively recent fruit in the southern hemisphere where we tend to think of blueberry muffins as being an American treat. However, locally grown blueberries are now available fresh and frozen and make another tasty jam.

2 kg blueberries
½ cup water
2 kg sugar
juice of 1 lemon

Cook the blueberries gently in a pan with the water until tender. Stir in the sugar until dissolved, add the lemon juice and boil fast until the jam will set when tested. It is a rich red colour with a pleasant sharp flavour.

Cherry Jam

Sour cherries make excellent jam but sweet cherry jam lacks flavour. The trees are beautiful with blossom in spring and richly coloured leaves in autumn but they only fruit well where winters are cold.

2 kg cherries
½ cup lemon juice
2 kg sugar

Stone the cherries, put the fruit and lemon juice in a pan and heat gently to extract the juice. Add some of the stones tied in muslin, bring the jam to the boil and cook until the fruit is soft. Stir in the sugar until dissolved then boil the jam fast until it will set when tested. Remove the bag of cherry stones and pour the jam into jars. This is a soft-set jam.

Raspberry Jam

I once spent the summer holidays picking a ton of raspberries — a wonderful working holiday and a marvellous opportunity to try every imaginable raspberry dish. Raspberry jam was then and still is, one of my firm favourites.

2 kg raspberries
2 kg sugar

Put the hulled raspberries in the preserving pan and heat slowly until the juice begins to run. Simmer the fruit for 5 minutes. Stir in the sugar and when it has dissolved bring the jam to a fast boil. Cook 3-5 minutes and test for setting. Try not to overboil this jam or the fine flavour of the fruit will be lost.

Apricot Jam

Apricots are my favourite fruit — there is something quite wonderful about the scent, colour, flavour and texture of a tree-ripened apricot which people living outside an apricot-growing area never experience. The jam, too, is special — lovely with scones and whipped cream and often used as a glaze on apple or other fruit tarts and flans.

2 kg apricots
2 cups water
juice of 1 lemon
2 kg sugar
½ cup blanched, slivered almonds

Stone the apricots, put them with the water and lemon juice into a large pan and bring to the boil, stirring. Cook gently until the fruit is tender, then stir in the sugar. When it has dissolved boil the jam quickly until it will set, adding the slivered almonds towards the end of cooking. When setting point is reached remove the jam from the heat and let it stand about 10 minutes before pouring into jars. Cover when cold.

Blackcurrant Jam

Blackcurrants have a very dominant flavour but they are also rich in vitamins. Their high concentration of vitamin C makes them a valuable tonic and they are both a medicine and a food.

1.5 kg blackcurrants
1 litre water
2.25 kg sugar

Remove all the stalks from the currants and wash and drain them. Put them in a pan with the water, bring to the boil and simmer until the fruit is soft. Add the sugar and stir until it is dissolved then bring to the boil and boil fast until it will set when tested.

Plum or Damson Jam

Any type of plum, except the very watery early fruit, can be made into jam. I particularly like greengage and other yellow-skinned, yellow-fleshed plum jams, and damson jam. Because plum trees often crop heavily plum jam was the universal jam of my childhood and was often used in shortbread cakes and rolypoly or jam roll puddings. This recipe works for all plum/damson jams.

2 kg plums
3 cups water
2 kg sugar
juice of 2 lemons

Count the plums into the pan and add the water. Bring to the boil, lower the heat and cook gently until the plums are soft. Add the sugar, stirring to dissolve it completely before bringing the jam to a rolling boil. Skim out the plum stones with a slotted spoon as they rise to the surface of the jam. Sieve to allow all the fruit to go back in the jam and count the stones to see that they equal the number of plums. Add the lemon juice, stir well and test for setting. When setting point is reached remove the jam from the heat. Use a plastic jug to pour the jam into warmed and dried jars and seal when cold.

Blackberry and Elderberry Jam

All through the blackberry season I pick billies full of fruit (and have stained fingers). I have a thornless black-berry in the garden but I always gather wild berries too. They make beautiful jam on their own but an even bet-ter jam mixed half and half with elderberries. (Don't forget to ask the elder's permission to pick the berries or misfortune may befall you!)

equal quantities of blackberries and elderberries
350 g sugar to every 500 g fruit

Weigh and wash the fruit and remove any stalks. Put it in a pan and mash slightly to start the juice flowing. Bring to the boil slowly and boil gently until the fruit is soft, about 15-20 minutes. Stir in the sugar until dissolved and boil until the jam will set.

Peach Jam

Peach jam should be made with yellow-fleshed peaches. It has a fine 'peachy' flavour and can be varied by adding 1 teaspoon per kg of cinnamon or ginger or $^1/_2$ tea-spoon of ground cloves or allspice. Almonds blanched and slivered are nice with peach jam too.

2 kg peaches
2 cups water
2 kg sugar
2 lemons
$^1/_4$ cup blanched, slivered almonds

Peel, stone and slice the peaches and cook with the wa-ter in a well buttered pan. When soft stir in the sugar, until it dissolves, add the lemon juice and almonds and boil hard, stirring often to prevent the jam sticking, until it will set.

Pear Ginger

The buttery texture and fine flavour of pears seems to be enhanced by two spices, ginger and cinnamon, and also by the clean tang of lemon. All these things to-gether make another favourite jam.

2 kg pears
2 lemons, zest and juice
2 cups crystallised ginger
2 kg sugar
pinch of cinnamon

Peel, core and chop the pears into a bowl, add the zest and juice of the lemons, the ginger, and mix in the sugar and cinnamon. Combine well and leave over-night. Next day, transfer to the pan and cook, stirring, until the mixture boils. Lower the heat and simmer until the jam will set.

Feijoa Jam

Some people dislike the appearance of feijoa jam because of its brown colour but it has a lovely rich flavour expecially when the fruit is cut into chunks. The rind of a Lisbon lemon pared with a zester and/ or some chopped crystallised ginger may be added to taste.

2 kg feijoas
$^1/_2$ cup water
2 kg sugar
juice of 2 lemons

Butter the bottom of the pan lightly to prevent the fruit sticking. Add peeled, sliced feijoas and water and boil, stirring, until the fruit is soft. Stir in the sugar until it dissolves, add the lemon juice and boil briskly until the jam will set. Allow to cool slightly before pouring into jars.

Instead of peeling, feijoas may be halved and the pulp scooped out with a strong teaspoon. Which-ever method you use, the fruit will stain your hands. Lemon juice and a little sugar will help remove any stains.

Kiwifruit Jam

For some reason kiwifruit jam resembles strawberry jam in flavour. It also combines well with other flavours and can be made with orange or pineapple juice instead of water. Two bananas peeled and sliced, or 2 tablespoons of crystallised ginger may be added to each 1 kg of cooked fruit, with the sugar, to make kiwifruit and banana or kiwifruit and ginger jam. The fruit should be ripe.

2 kg kiwifruit
2 cups water
juice of 1 lemon
1.75 kg sugar

Peel the kiwifruit and wash them carefully, to remove any bristles. Chop the fruit into a pan, add the water and lemon juice. Simmer until the fruit is tender, then mash it and stir in the sugar. Bring to the boil and boil fast until it will set. Allow to cool a little before potting. Cover when cold.

Cape Gooseberry Jam

Cape gooseberries really come from South America but were collected from Cape Town by colonists on their way to Australia and New Zealand and called after the Cape of Good Hope. Every garden had some in my childhood and they would be picked and saved for a week in their 'paper' cases to make a pot or two of jam.

1 kg Cape gooseberries
small amount of water
1 kg sugar

Remove the cases and wash and drain the fruit. Put them in a pan with just enough water to stop them sticking, bring to the boil and cook, stirring until they are soft, 7 - 10 minutes. Stir in sugar until dissolved, bring the jam to the boil again and boil fast 10 - 15 minutes until it will set.

JELLIES

There is something special about jellies — their clear, bright colour, the way they wobble on the spoon and the fresh sweet or tart taste. Mother made redcurrant, crab-apple and blackberry and apple jellies and I still use some of her heavy glass jelly jars, although little jars are more suitable because all the jelly can be eaten at one meal.

Jellies are easy to make but because there are two processes involved they take longer from start to finish than jams. As with making jam, the fruit should not be wet when picked. Rinse the fruit in cold water if it is dusty, then put the fruit in the pan and cover with cold water. Bring to the boil and simmer until the fruit is soft. Remove the pan from the heat.

Put the jelly bag, or cloth for straining the liquid through, into a basin and pour boiling water on it to scald it. Fish it out with the handle of a wooden spoon and, as soon as you can handle it, wring it out. Arrange it in a large sieve, strainer or colander over a large basin and pour the fruit and liquid from the pan into the jelly bag. (It is more controllable if you use the jug rather than tipping the hot liquid and fruit directly from the pan.) Then tie the top of the bag with a piece of strong string and suspend it from the back of a chair so that the remaining liquid can drip into the basin. Leave it overnight and never, never squeeze the juice out of the bag or your jelly will be dull and cloudy. If you are only making a small quantity the bag may hold it all just suspended in the sieve.

Next day measure the liquid back into the clean pan and add 2 cups of sugar to every 2½ cups of juice. Heat it slowly, stirring until the sugar is dissolved, then bring it to the boil and boil fast until the jelly will set when tested on a saucer. Lemon juice may be strained into the jelly to help it set. Once setting point is reached take the pan off the heat and skim off any froth carefully. Drain and dry the jars heated in hot water in the sink and use the jug to fill them. Pour the jelly in carefully,

tilting the jar to avoid lots of little air bubbles forming. Cover the jelly immediately if you are using a vacuum seal, otherwise stand the jars on a board and allow the jelly to get quite cold before covering with a cellophane jam cover. Label each jar with the name and date and store in a cool dark cupboard. If you do not use much jelly, pot it in small jars which can be used up in one or two meals. Jelly crystallises if it is left in the refrigerator for any length of time. The sweet jellies are used to spread on all sorts of breads and scones. Tart jellies are often eaten with meat, game or poultry and cheese.

Gooseberry and Elderflower Jelly

The elder is in flower when the gooseberries ripen and the fruit and flowers combine to make a delicately flavoured and coloured jelly often called Muscat Jelly because of its slightly grapey taste.

½ kg large green gooseberries
water
sugar
elderflowers

Top and tail the gooseberries, put them in a pan and barely cover them with water. Simmer until the fruit is cooked and strain overnight through a jelly bag. Next day measure the liquid into the pan and heat it. Stir in 2 cups of sugar for every 2½ cups of liquid until the sugar is dissolved, bring to the boil, then add 3 heads of elderflower snipped from their stalks for every 2½ cups of liquid. Infuse the elderflowers for about 5-10 minutes then strain them out and boil the jelly until it will set when tested. Pour into warm, dry jars and seal when cold.

Redcurrant Jelly

Redcurrants are glorious to look at, like clusters of clear ruby beads. Our next-door neighbours had a row of currant bushes along the path to the back door. As the fruit ripened they were draped with old net curtains to protect them from the birds, and the cat sat on the step ready to pounce. Currants are picked by the cluster and stripped into a basin with a silver fork if you are going to eat them or make a pudding, but they do not need to be stripped for jelly.

Simmer any quantity of redcurrants in a pan, just barely covered with water, for about 15-20 minutes to extract the juice. Strain through a jelly bag and leave to drip overnight. Next day measure the liquid into the pan and add 2 cups of sugar for every 2½ cups juice. Stir over a moderate heat to dissolve the sugar then bring to the boil and boil fast until the jelly will set. This takes only about 5 minutes because redcurrants are rich in pectin. Do not overcook redcurrant jelly at any stage or you can ruin its fine fresh flavour.

Blackberry or Blackberry and Apple Jelly

I love blackberry jam but for those who like the taste without the pips blackberry jelly is the answer. Apple readily takes on the flavour of the blackberries, makes small quantities go further, improves the taste and gives the jelly a better set. Any windfall apples will do, used in the proportion of 1 kg of apples to every 2 kg blackberries.

2 kg blackberries
water
1 kg apples
sugar

Just cover the blackberries with water and, if adding apples, slice them, don't bother to peel or core them. Boil gently until the fruit is soft and strain overnight through a jelly bag. Next day measure the liquid in the pan and heat it. Stir in 2 cups of sugar to every 2½ cups of liquid. Dissolve the sugar before raising the heat then boil fast until the jelly will set when tested, about 10 minutes. Pour into warm, dry jars and cover when cold.

Apple Jelly

Any windfall apples can be made into jelly. Sourish apples are the nicest to my taste and I use the rosy liquid combined with herbs such as mint, rosemary, and rose or peppermint geranium to vary the flavour.

Chop the apples roughly into the pan and cover with water. Bring to the boil and cook until the fruit is pulpy. Strain overnight through a jelly bag. Next day measure the liquid into the pan and heat it. Stir in 2 cups of sugar for every 2½ cups of liquid, and when it is dissolved boil fast until it will set when tested.

MINT JELLY: Cook a bunch of mint in with the sugar and liquid and add ½ cup of cider vinegar. When the jelly will set strain out the mint and add fresh chopped mint to taste. Heat it to boiling point again before pouring into warm, dry jars. Serve with meat.

ROSEMARY JELLY: Make apple jelly as usual and pour the hot jelly onto a sprig of rosemary in each jar. Do not wash the rosemary or pick it damp or the jelly may turn mouldy. Rosemary jelly may be served with lamb or eaten with rosemary scones.

ROSE GERANIUM JELLY: This is made in the same way by pouring the hot apple jelly into jars with one or two rose geranium leaves in each jar. I think 'Attar of Roses' (*Pelargonium capitatum*) gives the best rose flavour.

Any herb such as rosemary or rose geranium put in a jar and covered with boiling jelly will rise to the top of the jelly. It is a good idea to let the jelly cool a little and then hold the herb under with a fork until the jelly begins to set. Lift out the fork when the herbs stay down and seal when the jelly is cold.

Crab-apple Jelly

The small, tart crab-apples make a brilliant jewel-red jelly, either alone or combined with herbs such as mint. Many ornamental varieties are grown in gardens for the beauty of their spring blossom and autumn fruits. They crop heavily and can be made into jellies, wines and pickles. They are ripe when they begin to fall.

Put whole or chopped crab-apples into a pan and cover with water. Bring to the boil and simmer until the fruit is tender. Strain overnight through a jelly bag. Next day measure the liquid back into the pan and heat it. Stir in 2 cups of sugar for every 2½ cups of liquid and when it is dissolved bring to the boil and boil until the jelly will set. Pour into warm, dry jars and cover

when cold. Make mint or rosemary jelly using crab-apples in the same way as apples (*see* left).

Grape Jelly

When we pick grapes, all the odds and ends of fruit that fall off the bunches into the boxes are washed quickly and simmered up for jelly. The smell is divine! I particularly like jelly made from wine grapes and often make small pots of it poured onto sprigs of fresh thyme — the two robust flavours go well together. Because grape jelly does not set well on its own, it is a good idea to cook apples with the grapes to provide pectin, and to add lemon juice.

Strip the grapes from their stalks and measure into the pan. Add about one-third of the quantity of chopped cooking apples, for example, 2 cups of apple to 6 cups of grapes. Just cover with water, bring to the boil and simmer gently until the skins split and the liquid is a rich colour. Strain through a jelly bag overnight. Next day measure the liquid back into the pan and heat it. Stir in 2 cups of sugar to every 2½ cups of liquid and when it is dissolved add the juice of 2 lemons and boil fast until it will set when tested. Pour into warmed, dry jars, with or without a sprig or two of thyme in them, and cover when cold.

Quince Jelly

This large, downy, yellow fruit is extremely hard and wonderfully aromatic. Before using, always wipe the skins to remove any down. If you don't wish to eat the quinces after they've been used for jelly-making, they can be chopped up, skin, cores and all. If you wish to eat the fruit after the liquid has been strained out, peel and core quinces and slice them into the pan. The skins and cores should be tied in a muslin bag and cooked with the fruit to improve the colour of the jelly.

quinces
1 litre water to every 500 g fruit
sugar

Prepare the quinces and weigh them. Put in a pan with 1 litre of water to every 500 g of fruit, add the skins and cores in a muslin bag and bring to the boil. Cook steadily, without stirring, until the fruit is soft. Drain through a fine sieve, measure and add 2 cups of sugar to every 2½ cups of liquid. Bring to the boil, stirring to dissolve the sugar, and boil fast until the jelly will set. The quince slices may be eaten with cream, yoghurt or custard, or used in a pie or crumble.

No-strain Quince Jelly

In old jam recipe books there are often several recipes for the same thing with slight variations. This is a real two-in-one recipe best undertaken when you have lots of time because a whole quince takes longer to become tender.

6 large ripe quinces
2 kg sugar
3 litres water
juice of 2 lemons

Choose 6 perfect quinces and wash them. Leave them whole. Make a syrup by stirring the sugar into the water until it is dissolved. Add the quinces and strained lemon juice, bring gradually to the boil and boil until the jelly will set when tested. Remove the quinces carefully and pour the jelly into warmed, dry jars. Eat the fruit, warm or cold, with cream.

Guava Jelly

The cherry or strawberry guava, *Psidium cattleianum*, is native to Brazil but grows easily in warm climates and has lots of small, round, red–wine–coloured fruit which ripen towards the end of autumn. They drop easily and make a fruity carpet under the tree. When freshly gathered they make a dark red jelly with a distinctive flavour to serve with breads, meat, or cheese and crackers.

2.5 *kg guavas*
10 *cups water*
sugar
juice of 1 lemon

Put the guavas in a pan with the water and simmer about 30 minutes. Stand 15 minutes and then strain overnight through a jelly bag. Next day measure the liquid back into the pan and heat it. Add 2 cups of sugar to every 2½ cups of liquid. Add the strained lemon juice. Stir to dissolve the sugar, bring the jelly to the boil and boil fast until it will set when tested. Pour into warmed, dry jars and cover when cold.

Rowan Jelly

The rowan is a tree of ancient magical association often planted as a protection against witches and fairies. It is also very beautiful and, like so many of our fruits, a member of the rose family. The berries which ripen in late summer can be made into a tart jelly with apples or crab-apples. It tastes good with venison or game.

2 *kg rowan berries*
1 *kg apples or crab-apples*
water
sugar

Wash the fruit, strip the rowan berries from their stalks and chop the apples or crab-apples roughly. Put them in a pan and just cover with water. Bring to the boil and cook until soft. Strain overnight through a jelly bag. Next day measure the liquid into the pan and add 2 cups of sugar to every 2½ cups of liquid. Heat and stir to dissolve the sugar, then boil fast until the jelly will set. Pour into warmed, dry jars and cover when cold.

Elderberry and apple or crab-apple jelly can be made in the same way.

Medlar Jelly

The medlar is an old-fashioned tonic fruit that is entirely brown and although it should be picked while the fruit is still firm, it must be 'bletted' or left to soften completely before it can be eaten raw or cooked. The medlar ripens late and is often left on the tree until after a frost or two. We have blackbird problems so generally have to pick them earlier. They keep well, stored in single or double layers in shallow boxes.

Put soft, ripe medlars whole into a pan and just cover with water. Cook gently until the fruit is pulpy. Strain through a double layer of muslin in a sieve into a basin. When the dripping ceases, measure the liquid into the pan and heat it. Stir in 2 cups of sugar to every 2½ cups of liquid. Add the strained juice of a lemon or orange. Heat, stirring until the sugar is dissolved, then boil fast until the jelly will set when tested. Pour into warmed, dry jars and cover when cold.

While you are heating the liquid in the pan, tip the strained fruit out of the muslin and push it through a large mesh sieve to remove the skins and pips. Store the pulp in the refrigerator to make paste, cakes and tarts.

MARMALADES

Marmalade gets its name from the Portuguese word *marmelo*, a quince. Marmalade was originally a sort of quince paste (*see* page 33) which was solid enough to be cut with a knife and eaten as a dessert. It was imported into England from Portugal as early as the fifteenth century and, as people experimented with sugar and fruit, 'marmalade' was used to describe pastes of other fruits [e.g. 'marmelett of cherys, marmelett of aprecocks']. At this time sweet oranges were not known in Europe, only the bitter Seville type, and when cooks

began to flavour apple jelly with bitter orange rind and juice, marmalade as we know it began to be made. It was not until the early nineteenth century that it was used as a spread, 'an admirable and nutritious substitute for butter', and eaten for breakfast rather than for dinner.

The first marmalade I remember was made by my mother, who used the universal New Zealand recipe made with Poorman's oranges, a bitter type of grapefruit that makes excellent marmalade. (A breakfast cup was a larger teacup and any cup that lost its handle by being knocked in the sink while washing up ended up serving as a measure). Her recipe is:

4 *large Poorman's oranges*
2 *lemons*
12 *breakfast cups water*
12 *breakfast cups sugar*

Slice the fruit finely with a sharp knife on a wooden board, removing and keeping the pips separate. Put the sliced fruit in a large basin, cover with the water and add the pips tied in a piece of muslin. Soak overnight. Next day pour the mixture into the preserving pan, bring it to the boil and boil for 20 minutes. Remove the muslin bag of pips and stir in the sugar until dissolved. Bring the marmalade back to the boil and boil until it will set when tested.

This is a fine flavoured jelly marmalade and mother made several batches to last through the year. (If it ran out, plum jam was served for breakfast.) As grapefruit were 'improved' and had smoother skins, darker colour and fewer pips, people used them instead of the sourer Poorman's orange and, now, grapefruit marmalade is *the* marmalade commonly made in New Zealand.

When I came to live here there was a Poorman's orange tree in the orchard and 30 years and many pots of marmalade later, it is still alive and bearing.

However, I was also very fond of lime marmalade, so we planted Tahitian limes and then the sour mandarin, the kumquat and, finally, Seville orange trees, so now we can have any sour sort of marmalade we like to make. I use the same recipe for all types and find it never fails. I also slice the fruit finely with my grandmother's knife because that is how I like it but of course it can be minced or chopped in a food processor.

grapefruit or kumquats or limes or Seville oranges
water
sugar

Slice the fruit finely, removing and discarding any pips. Weigh the fruit, put it in a basin and cover it with 3 times the fruit's weight in water; for example, if you have 1 kg of fruit, cover it with approximately 3 litres

water. Soak it overnight. Next day tip the fruit and water into the preserving pan and bring it to the boil. Cook it steadily until the rind is tender and transparent. Then measure the mixture and stir in ¾ cup of sugar to every cup of pulp. Return it to the pan, stir until the sugar is dissolved, and bring to the boil. Boil fast until it will set when tested. Pour into pots and seal when cold. If you want a thicker marmalade add only 2 litres of water for every 1 kg of fruit.

Grapefruit marmalade is clear and pale. Kumquat marmalade is clear and orange. Lime marmalade is cloudy (as is lemon marmalade) and pale. Seville orange marmalade is partly cloudy, partly clear, and orange but not so brilliant in colour as kumquat.

Any mixture of citrus fruit can be used to taste but do soak it, as the soaking softens the peel and speeds the cooking. The large quantity of water allows for some to boil off while the fruit is softening.

Quince Marmalade

The other type of marmalade we make is quince marmalade — not so thick as the paste but still a delicious firm conserve.

2 *kg quinces*
2 *lemons*
2 *litres water*
2.5 *kg sugar*

Rub the down from the quince skins, peel, core, and slice the fruit finely. Remove the rind from the lemons with a zester or grater, and simmer the fruit, rind and water in a large pan until tender. Add the lemon juice and stir in the sugar until dissolved. Bring to the boil and boil fast, until it will set when tested. Pour into jars and seal when cold.

This tastes more like jam than marmalade but it never lasts long! It may be eaten for breakfast, lunch or dinner but I like it best on toast.

FRUIT AND NUT BUTTERS, CURDS AND PASTES

All sorts of delicious spreads or sweetmeats may be made by cooking fruit and sugar slowly together until a thick butter or paste is formed. Sometimes eggs are added or fruits combined with nuts but, however they are made, these treats can be enjoyed often for very little trouble.

Damson Cheese

The tart flavour and rich red colour of damson cheese make it attractive both to eat and to look at. Other plums may be used in the same way and so may apricots or peaches. As with making other pastes and spreads, constant stirring is the secret of success.

1.5 kg damsons
½ cup water
sugar

Put the damsons and water in a saucepan and simmer until they are soft. Then tip them into a sieve and push the pulp through, discarding stones and skins. Measure the pulp back into the pan and stir in 1 cup of sugar for each 1 cup of pulp and stir and heat until the sugar is dissolved. Continue to cook and stir until the mixture is thick and, like paste, comes away from the sides of the pan. Pour into buttered dishes and spread out about 1cm thick. Dry as for quince paste (*see* page 33).

Blackberry Cheese

While damson cheese and quince paste have very strong, almost aggressive flavours, blackberry cheese is milder and more subtle. I expect the blending of cooking apples and the resulting pectin also makes it more digestable. It may be served with bread or crackers like a very thick jam or cut in slices and eaten with meat.

1 kg blackberries
500 g cooking apples
water
500 g sugar to every 500 g pulp

Put the washed blackberries and chopped, but unpeeled, apples in a saucepan and simmer in water to cover. Sieve the fruit to remove pips and skin, weigh the pulp and mix with an equal weight of sugar. Heat and stir well to dissolve the sugar, bring to the boil and boil gently until the mixture is very thick. Put in wide-mouthed jars. Cover when cold and store 2–3 months to mature.

Lemon Curd, Lemon Honey, Lemon Cheese

All three names are used for this delicious, lemony sweet spread. We used to make it in spring when the hens began to lay more eggs than we needed but it can be made at any time of year. The sour Lisbon lemons with their tangy juice are better than the sweeter Meyer lemons.

4 eggs
125 g butter
250 g sugar
2 lemons

Beat the eggs in a basin, add the chopped butter, sugar and the finely grated rind and strained juice of the lemons. Stand the basin in a saucepan of nearly boiling water and stir the mixture until it thickens, or cook it in the top of a double boiler. Pot into small jars and seal with vacuum lids and the lemon honey will keep well. Use as a spread on breads and scones, or as a cake or tart filling.

Lime Butter

Tahitian limes are easily grown in subtropical climates and provide a pleasant alternative to lemons in drinks, fish and chicken dishes and marmalades. They are also excellent in sweet dishes and lime butter can be used like lemon curd as a spread, cake or tart filling or even as a hot sauce for sponge-type puddings.

3 eggs
125 g butter
2 cups sugar
½ cup lime juice

Beat the eggs in a basin, add chopped butter, sugar and strained lime juice. Cook, stirring, in the top of a double boiler over simmering water, until the mixture is thick and smooth. If you wish, add some lime zest as well. Put in small jars and store in the refrigerator.

Apple Butter

A well flavoured apple is best for making apple butter otherwise the taste is too bland. I favour an old-fashioned Northern Spy — a variety known for its vigour and formerly used as a root stock — which is an excellent apple for eating raw or cooking. Golden Delicious also make good apple butter. Spices can be added to taste and if the fruit is really ripe hardly any sugar is needed, so taste as you go — but don't burn your tongue.

2 kg apples
1 cup water
1 cup sugar
juice and rind of 1 lemon

Chop the apples roughly and simmer gently with the water in the pan until they are quite soft. Sieve the fruit, return the pulp to the pan and discard pips and skin. Cook the pulp gently until thick, stirring all the time

to prevent it burning at the bottom. Add the sugar and lemon and continue to cook and stir until all the liquid is absorbed. Pour into jars and cover when cold.

Spiced Apple or Crab-apple Butter

This is a good way to use the pulp left over after making jelly. If the jelly is strained through a sieve lined with muslin the apples or crab-apples can be used straight away instead of getting too dry overnight in the jelly bag. Different sorts of crab-apples are more or less sour so taste the butter as you stir and add more or less sugar.

5 cups crab-apple pulp
5 cups (or more) sugar
1 teaspoon cinnamon
1 teaspoon allspice
juice of 1 lemon

Sieve the pulp to remove skins, cores, pips and stalks and measure it into a preserving pan. Stir in the sugar, spices and lemon juice and heat gently, stirring all the time to dissolve the sugar. Bring to the boil and cook and stir until the mixture thickens and comes away from the sides of the saucepan. Pot in small jars, being careful to exclude air pockets, and cover when cold. Spices may be varied to taste.

Passionfruit Butter

When I was small we had an enormous passionfruit vine all over the wall of the shed. We picked the fruit up by the clothes-basketful and ate them alone and in combination with all sorts of peach, pear, apple and banana desserts. This passionfruit spread was a favourite on bread and as a cake filling.

2 eggs
50 g butter
1 cup sugar
6 passionfruit
2 lemons

Beat the eggs, add the chopped butter, sugar, passionfruit pulp, the grated rind of 1 lemon and the strained juice of 2 lemons. Put in the top of a double boiler and heat over simmering water, stirring till thick. Pour into small pots and cover when cold.

Quince Paste

This is my favourite quince dish, and whatever else I do with quinces I always make at least one dish full. It is a real Arabian Nights delight, sweet yet tart, sticky yet smooth, and the almonds are the finishing touch.

2 kg quinces
10 cups water
1.5 kg sugar
½ cup chopped blanched almonds

Peel, core and slice the quinces into a saucepan. Add the peels tied in muslin, cover with the water, bring to the boil and cook until the fruit is tender. Remove the bag and strain the quinces, retaining the liquid. Put 1 cup of liquid back in the pan and stir in the sugar. When it boils add 1 cup of sieved quince pulp. Continue to stir in 1 cup of liquid to every 1 cup of sieved pulp until all the pulp is back in the pan. Simmer and stir until it is thick like dough and watch it carefully so that it does not burn. Then add the chopped almonds, mix well and pour the pulp out into well buttered dishes or shallow trays and spread it out about 1 cm thick. Dry it in the sun or in a cool oven or the hot water cupboard. Watch out for ants, flies and mice which enjoy the almonds! When it is quite firm cut it into squares or diamonds with a hot knife. It may be brushed

with brandy or rosewater and sprinkled with castor sugar and/or cinnamon then stored between layers of waxed paper with fresh bay leaves in shallow boxes. Serve it with coffee or cream cheese as a sweetmeat.

Medlar Paste

The pulp left from making medlar jelly is excellent for making paste as long as it is sieved almost immediately the liquid for the jelly has dripped out, otherwise it dries quickly and is much harder to sieve. Orange zest or thin strips of orange or mandarin peel and ground cloves are good flavours to add.

equal weights of medlar pulp and sugar
1-2 oranges or 3-6 mandarins
medlar pulp
ground cloves

Sieve the medlars and weigh the pulp into the pan. Stir in an equal weight of sugar and add the juice and rind of the oranges or mandarins to taste. Heat and cook, stirring constantly, until the pulp is thick and comes away from the sides of the pan. Add ground cloves to taste, mix well and pour out onto a well buttered dish or tray. Dry and store in the same way as quince paste.

What wondrous life is this I lead!
Ripe apples drop about my head;
The luscious clusters of the vine
Upon my mouth do crush their wine;
The nectarine and curious peach
Into my hands themselves do reach;
Stumbling on melons, as I pass,
Ensnared with flowers, I fall on grass . . .
    Andrew Marvell

Chutneys, Pickles, & SAUCES

In past times when cooking equipment consisted of an iron pot hung on a chain over an open fire, most ingredients had to be cooked together. Meat, vegetables, cereals, fresh and dried fruits and seasonings were all put in the same pot so that the taste/flavour was somewhat sweet and sour. As kitchen equipment became more sophisticated, different courses could be separated and savoury foods could be served as well as sweet foods and sweet and sour foods. Now most first courses are savoury and most dessert courses are sweet and we compensate for the loss of sweet and sour cookery by accompanying our savoury courses with either sour, or sweet and sour pickles, sauces or chutneys.

The use of salt for preserving foods is as old as history. Vinegar was also an ancient seasoning and the combination of brined vegetables and/or fruit, washed, drained and preserved in spiced vinegars, with meats, salads or just bread and cheese, is delicious. These pickles stimulate the appetite, and the rich, sweet and sour fruitiness of a plum or tomato sauce or the spicy hotness of chutney has a similar effect. So, simply by opening a jar you can transform an everyday meal into a special treat.

CHUTNEYS

Basic Chutney Recipe

Larousse says that chutney 'is a condiment of Indian origin' originally made with mangoes. However, as mangoes did not grow in England, Mrs Beeton's 'Bengal Recipe for making Mango Chutney' substituted apples. Other fruits that pulp down well may also be used, such as peaches, plums, feijoas, and this good basic recipe may be used with any fruit you choose. Chutneys are sweeter than pickles, having fruit, sugar and sultanas in them. If you want a sourer chutney, add a little less sugar but watch its keeping quality: too little sugar and chutney will 'go off' sooner rather than later. Fresh garlic and ginger give a 'hot' enough flavour for me but chillies may be added if you wish.

2 kg apples, feijoas or other fruit
1 kg brown sugar
750 g sultanas
250 g garlic
500 g fresh ginger
2 tablespoons salt or to taste
1.5-2 litres vinegar

Peel and chop the apples and put in a large saucepan with the sugar, sultanas and whole unpeeled garlic cloves and beaten fresh ginger tied in muslin. Add the salt and stir in the vinegar. Bring to the boil and cook, stirring occasionally, until the mixture is pulpy and thick. Remove the muslin bag, discard the ginger but pop the garlic out of its papery skin, mash it and stir it into the chutney. Pour into jars and vacuum seal. This chutney will improve with keeping.

Orange Ginger Chutney

Orange and ginger are complementary flavours and this chutney goes well with duck and Chinese or Southeast Asian foods, rice and curries. It is quick and simple to make.

4 oranges
2 apples
1 onion
125 g crystallised ginger
1 tablespoon plain salt
1 tablespoon mustard powder or seeds
2 cups vinegar
1 cup brown sugar

Peel and chop the oranges, apples and onion. Slice the ginger. Combine all ingredients in a saucepan, bring to the boil and simmer slowly for 1½ hours. Bottle and seal while hot.

Uncooked Apple Chutney

One day long ago someone came to buy a case of Granny Smith apples to make chutney. 'That's a lot of apple chutney,' I said. 'Yes,' she replied, 'but we all like uncooked apple chutney.' I asked for the recipe and next day it was in the apple box at the gate. Every year since then I've made this wonderful recipe. It will keep for a year (if no one eats it).

25 g garlic
1 kg tart apples
1 kg dried fruit (e.g. sultanas, raisins)
1 kg brown sugar
125 g mixed peel
1 tablespoon plain salt
1 tablespoon mixed spice
pinch of cloves and cinnamon
pepper to taste
malt vinegar

Mince the peeled garlic and peeled, cored apples and dried fruit. Put in a large basin and add all the other ingredients using sufficient vinegar to bring it to the desired consistency. Cover with a cloth. Stand the chutney at room temperature and stir several times daily for three days. Bottle and cover. Keep in a cool, dark cupboard. Serve with bread and cheese, cold meats and salads. Do not substitute onions for garlic because onions ferment and will spoil the chutney.

Feijoa Chutney

Anyone with a feijoa tree knows that when the fruit begins to fall there is a huge quantity to deal with. Feijoas are a very adaptable fruit and make excellent jam, wine, puddings and chutneys. The fruit can either be peeled or cut in half and the flesh scooped out with a teaspoon. Preparing feijoas stains your hands. Lemon juice helps to whiten them afterwards.

1.5 kg feijoas
1 kg onions
½ cup crystallised ginger
2 cups sultanas
2 cups brown sugar
1 teaspoon ground cloves
3 teaspoons curry powder
2 tablespoons salt
1 litre malt vinegar

Peel and chop the feijoas and onions and slice the ginger finely. Combine all ingredients in a large pan and bring to the boil, stirring. Simmer until thick, then pour into jars. Seal when cold.

Tamarillo Chutney

The tamarillo was always known as a tree tomato when I was small and they can be skinned in the same way as tomatoes by covering them with boiling water for a few minutes. Red ones look best but yellow ones are sweeter. They can be used in all sorts of sweet and savoury dishes.

1.5 kg tamarillos
500 g onions
500 g apples
½ cup crystallised ginger
2 cups vinegar
2 cups brown sugar
½ teaspoon cayenne pepper
12 cloves
12 peppercorns

Peel and chop the tamarillos, onions and apples and put them in a large pan with all the other ingredients plus the cloves and peppercorns tied in muslin. Bring to the boil, stirring, and cook until the mixture is thick. Pour into jars and seal when cold. 1 tablespoon of mixed spice can be used in place of cloves and pepper.

Indian Peach Chutney

This recipe comes from a Mrs Brocket. It was one she always made and which everyone enjoyed. Peaches have a lovely texture for chutney and can be left in medium-sized chunks so that their flavour comes through with the ginger.

1.5 kg peaches
1.5 kg sugar
1 dessertspoon ground ginger
1 dessertspoon salt
1½ red chillies tied in muslin (or well crushed)
3 cups malt vinegar
2 grated apples
3 finely chopped onions

Gently simmer the peaches and sugar together, stirring to avoid burning, until they are jammy. Add the remaining ingredients, stir well and boil until the chutney is thick. Pour into jars and seal when cold.

FRESH CHUTNEYS AND DRESSINGS

Certain combinations of fruits and/or vegetables, sometimes with yoghurt or coconut added, are traditionally used as side dishes to accompany 'hot' food such as curry. The simplest of these dishes is sliced

banana with grated coconut or coconut cream but there are lots of other delicious and quickly made fresh chutneys.

Fresh Apple Chutney

2 cm peeled root ginger
3 crushed cloves garlic
1-2 green chillies, deseeded
3 sprigs mint, finely chopped
½ teaspoon salt
2 apples
lemon juice

Crush ginger, garlic, chillies and mint together and add salt, grated apples and lemon juice to keep the apple white and give the right consistency. Alternatively, blend all the ingredients in a blender. Serve with curry and rice or lentil dishes.

Cucumber and Yoghurt

Finely slice cucumbers, sprinkle with salt and stand for 30 minutes. Drain off the liquid, put the slices in a dish and cover with plain yoghurt sprinkled with fresh, finely chopped mint.

Fresh Kiwifruit Chutney

Peel and slice ripe kiwifruit and sprinkle with lemon juice to taste. Add a garnish of diced sweet red pepper and serve with curry.

Fresh Nectarine Chutney

1 cup finely chopped celery
1 cup finely chopped nectarines
1 tablespoon lemon juice

Combine all ingredients and toss well. A little cucumber or capsicum may be added to taste.

Fresh Mint Chutneys

These herb and spice chutneys are particularly tasty and cooling with hot spicy foods like curry or kebabs. They also taste good with lamb dishes. Fresh coriander leaves may be used in place of, or combined with, mint to taste. They are best made in a blender.

RECIPE ONE
½ litre plain yoghurt
1 small, finely chopped onion
1-2 cloves garlic
1½ teaspoons cumin or caraway seeds
3 tablespoons chopped mint

Mix together and serve chilled.

RECIPE TWO
1 cup finely chopped mint or coriander leaves
8 finely chopped shallots
1 clove garlic, crushed with
1 teaspoon salt
2 teaspoons sugar
1 teaspoon garam masala
4 teaspoons lemon juice
2 tablespoons water

Combine all ingredients in a blender till smooth. Cover and chill before serving.

PICKLES

My father loved small water cracker biscuits topped with gherkins and cheese and every year he grew enough gherkins to make 6-10 jars full. He would pick them at the size he liked, then rub the bristles off, brew the spiced vinegar and cook them until they were to his satisfaction. For a long time blades of mace were hard to get but now they are usually available and add a lovely flavour.

1 kg gherkins to 1 litre of brine

Brine:
4 tablespoons salt to 1 litre cold water

4 cloves
2 teaspoons peppercorns
2 teaspoons allspice
2 blades mace
1 litre malt vinegar

Rub the bristles off the gherkins, cover them in brine and soak for three days. Drain them, dry them with a cloth and pack them into jars. Boil the spices in the vinegar gently for 10 minutes. Pour hot over the gherkins, cover them and leave for 24 hours. Drain and reboil the vinegar and pour it over the gherkins again each day for several days until they turn a good green. If the vinegar diminishes, add more. Finally seal and store in a cool, dark cupboard.

Pickled Figs

Towards the end of summer figs seem to just hang on the trees without getting properly ripe. This pickle is a delicious way to use them and I generally serve it as a dessert with whipped cream. It can also be served with cold meats.

3 cups white wine or cider vinegar
2 kg raw sugar
2 tablespoons cloves
50 g root ginger
4 kg figs

Combine the vinegar and sugar in a large saucepan and bring it to the boil, stirring to dissolve the sugar. Add the cloves and bruised root ginger tied in muslin and the whole figs. Cook very slowly for 1-2 hours, turning the figs gently with a slotted spoon. Remove the bag of spices. Pour into small jars which have been soaked in hot water and dried, and overflow with liquid and seal. Keep opened jars in the refrigerator.

Pickled Mandarins

Some seasons the Clementine trees are covered with very small fruit that is fiddly to peel, and no one can be bothered eating them. However, they are easy to pickle and make an interesting side dish with meat or can be used as a dessert or ice-cream topping with a little brandy or orange liqueur added.

1 kg Clementine mandarins
1 kg sugar
4 cups water
1½ cups cider vinegar
10 cm cinnamon stick
1½ teaspoons allspice
1½ teaspoons cloves

Prick the mandarins with a needle to prevent them bursting, drop them into a pan of boiling water and cook for 2-3 minutes. Drain them and discard the water. Combine the sugar and water in a saucepan, stirring to dissolve the sugar as it heats. Add the drained mandarins and cook until the fruit begins to look transparent. Remove from the heat, put the lid on the saucepan and stand overnight. Next day drain the mandarins out of the syrup and combine it with the vinegar and spices. Bring it to the boil and cook for 2-3 minutes. Then pour the boiling liquid over the mandarins, cover them and leave them overnight. Repeat this for 4 days. On the fourth day pack the fruit into dry, warmed jars, strain the spices out of the liquid, bring it to the boil, fill and overflow the jars and seal.

Pickled Beetroot

Beetroot was eaten with cold beef or corned beef at least once a week at home so my father grew a lot of it and mother always preserved it in large jars. I like this particular recipe she used because it is not too vinegary.

beetroot
water

pickling liquid:
1 *cup raw sugar*
1 *cup malt vinegar*
1 *cup water*
1 *teaspoon plain salt*
1 *teaspoon ground cinnamon*

Wash the beetroot and cut the leaves off about 5 cm from the roots. Put them in a large pan, cover with water and cook them whole. When they are tender drain the water off and leave the beetroot to cool, then slip their skins off and slice.

Make up the pickling liquid in sufficient quantity for the amount of beetroot, following the proportions above, bring it to the boil and boil for 5 minutes before adding the sliced beetroot. Bring it to the boil again and cook a further 5 minutes. Then pour the beetroot and its liquid into warmed, dried jars, overflow with liquid and seal. Keep opened jars in the refrigerator.

Spiced Peaches

This should be made with small, whole, yellow peaches or peacherines. It is a lovely pickle but watch carefully as you make it as the peaches disintegrate if they are cooked too long.

1.5 *kg small ripe peaches*
1 *clove for each peach*
2 *cups water*
4 *cups sugar*
½ *teaspoon cinnamon*
½ *teaspoon ginger*
1 *cup white wine vinegar*

Peel the peaches and stick a clove into each one. Combine the water and sugar in a saucepan, stirring to dissolve the sugar and bring it to the boil. Add the spices and peaches and cook gently for 10 minutes. Leave to cool. When cold drain the syrup into a saucepan, add the vinegar and simmer for 20 minutes. Add the peaches and cook until just tender. Remove from the heat, cover and leave overnight. Next day pack the peaches into small, warmed, dry jars. Reheat the syrup and pour, boiling, over the peaches. Overflow and seal. Keep opened jars in the refrigerator.

Bean Pickle

This is a good recipe to deal with a glut of beans. It creates something between mayonnaise and piccalilli, quite sweet but very tasty especially with cold meats and winter salads.

2 *kg sliced beans*
6 *sliced onions*
1 *large cup plain white flour*
½ *cup mustard powder*
2 *cups sugar*
1 *teaspoon ground pepper*

1 *teaspoon turmeric*
1 *egg*
4 *cups vinegar*
1¼ *cups water*
50 *g butter*

Cook the beans in a little water until almost tender. Add the finely sliced onions and boil 2-3 minutes. Stand 5 minutes and drain well. Combine dry ingredients and mix to a smooth paste with the beaten egg and a little vinegar. Heat the remaining vinegar and water, add the butter and stir in the thickening. Keep stirring to prevent it going lumpy as it comes to the boil. When the mixture thickens add the drained beans and onion and stir and cook until it boils again. Pour into warm, dry jars and cover when cold.

Cucumber Pickle

This is a favourite bread and butter pickle. It has a fresh flavour and is quick and easy to make. Generally I use long green cucumbers but I have used apple cucumbers successfully too. The peppers and garlic can be omitted if you wish.

4 *kg medium sized cucumbers*
6 *medium onions*
2 *green peppers*
3 *cloves garlic*
3 *tablespoons plain salt*
1 *litre cold water*
5 *cups sugar*
5 *cups cider vinegar*
2 *tablespoons mustard seeds*
1½ *teaspoons turmeric*

Do not peel the cucumbers, just slice them finely. Slice the onions and the peppers and tie the garlic in muslin. Make a brine with the salt and cold water and soak all the vegetables in it in a basin for 3 hours. Drain them well and put in a preserving pan with the remaining ingredients. Heat to boiling, stirring gently to dissolve the sugar. Remove the garlic, pour into warmed, dried jars and vacuum seal immediately.

Pickled Salad

This is a great idea for summer evenings when the lettuce has gone to seed and you want a salad but have forgotten to buy the ingredients. It can be eaten the day it is made but it improves with keeping and will last quite well if it gets the chance.

1 *cabbage*
1 *whole head of celery*
3 *green peppers*
brine of ½ cup salt and 1 litre cold water
2 *cups sugar*
1 *teaspoon mustard powder*
1 *teaspoon celery salt*
1 *cup water*
4 *cups white wine vinegar*

Quarter the cabbage, trimming off tough leaves and cutting out the stem, and chop it finely. String and chop the celery stalks finely too. Halve, deseed and slice the peppers. Put them all in a large bowl and cover with the brine. Stir well and leave 2 hours. Combine the sugar and spices and mix to a smooth paste with 1 cup of water in a saucepan. Stir in the vinegar and bring to the boil. Remove from the stove and cool. Drain the vegetables, wash them and drain throughly and fill large glass jars with the mixture. Pour in the cool spiced vinegar and cover with plastic lids. Gently tip the jars to remove any air bubbles. Store in the refrigerator. To serve, remove salad from the liquid with a slotted spoon into a dish.

Pickled Red Cabbage

Red cabbage is a very dense vegetable and pickles well for winter salads. Be careful to make sure that it is not too tightly packed in the jars so that no air is trapped in the leaves after the vinegar is added.

1 *red cabbage*
salt to taste
2 *bay leaves*
1 *clove garlic* } to each jar
peppercorns to taste
spiced vinegar

Cut the cabbage in quarters and remove tough outer leaves and central core. Wash and shred the cabbage finely, put in a basin and sprinkle plain salt over each layer. Leave overnight. Next day rinse and drain it thoroughly. Pack the cabbage loosely into the jars, adding a sliced clove of garlic, 2 bay leaves broken in pieces and a few peppercorns to each jar among the layers of cabbage. Pour in cold spiced vinegar (*see* page 44) to cover and seal with a plastic lid. Ready to eat after 48 hours.

Pickled Olives

More than a century ago my great-grandmother made a pilgrimage to the 'Holy Places', riding on a camel from Baghdad to Bethlehem and Jerusalem. One of the souvenirs of her adventure was a small candlestick of olive wood from the Mount of Olives. We have several olive trees and I love the silvery green of their leaves. We also love pickled olives. It is not difficult to pickle olives and there are a variety of ways to do this including one using lye or caustic soda which works well. However I now use a simpler method using brine.

Pick the olives when they are still green but just beginning to colour at the tip and put them into a

bucket half full of water so that they don't bruise and wash them well. Drain them. Make a brine in the proportion of 45 g salt, (3 tablespoons) to 1500 ml water, (12 ½ cups) and bring to the boil, stirring to dissolve the salt. Drop the olives into the boiling brine, bring it back to the boil and boil for 1 minute. Drain the olives and allow them to dry. Reserve the brine and allow it to go cold. Pack the olives into a large clean jar, or jars, and cover with the brine to which should be added:

*2 cups white wine or one each of wine
and tarragon vinegar
2 Lisbon lemons, sliced
6 cloves of garlic, peeled and sliced
2 tablespoons cumin seeds, crushed
2 tablespoons dried oregano*

Make sure that the olives are completely covered with liquid and then pour over enough olive oil to cover the surface. Cover the jars with plastic lids and store in a cool place. Leave at least a month and then taste an olive. I find that at first they are quite salty and bitter, especially around the stone, but they gradually improve and after several months taste very good indeed. Sometimes a slight scum develops on the top of the jars but the olives remain fine underneath the scum as long as they are covered. The lemon, herbs and vinegar give them an interesting flavour.

Jerusalem Artichoke Pickle

Jerusalem artichokes are really members of the sunflower family and come from South America, not Israel. They have tuberous roots which are an acquired taste — you either love or hate them. They are also extremely prolific and once they are in your garden they are there for ever. They make delicious soup and souffle, and are also excellent pickled — nice and crunchy.

*½ kg Jerusalem artichokes
1 onion per jar
1.5 litres white wine vinegar
750 g sugar
1 tablespoon turmeric
2 teaspoons mustard
2 teaspoons celery seeds
1 stick cinnamon
2.5 cm green ginger root*

Scrub and peel the artichokes and pack them whole into jars with one peeled onion sliced in rings per jar. Combine the vinegar, sugar and spices in a pan, heat, stirring to dissolve the sugar, and simmer for 30 minutes. Cool the pickling liquid and then pour it over the artichokes and onion and cover with plastic lids.

Spiced Vinegar

Homemade pickling spice is easy to make, as follows. The spiced vinegar can be used in many pickle recipes.

*2 tablespoons each whole allspice and crushed bay leaves
2 teaspoons each dill seeds, fennel seeds, small chillies
1 tablespoon each mustard seeds, black peppercorns
1 teaspoon whole cloves
5-7 cm cinnamon bark, crushed
vinegar*

Mix together well and store in a screw-topped glass jar. Use 2 tablespoons of pickling spice to every 1 litre of vinegar, bring to the boil then cover and infuse until cold. Strain out the spices before using it in fish or meat dishes, sauces, chutneys or pickles.

Jan's Dill Pickles

This is a recipe from an American friend which is quite easy to make and really tastes good.

cucumbers
1 litre spiced vinegar
¾ cup plain salt
2 litres boiling water

Cover whole cucumbers with cold water and leave overnight. Next day drain well and slice large cucumbers but leave small ones whole. Heat the pickling liquid until it is boiling. Wash and dry the jars and while they are still hot put 1-2 cloves of garlic and a sprig of dill in each. Pack in the cucumbers and cover with the boiling liquid, overflow and seal. Malt vinegar, cider vinegar or white wine vinegar may be used.

Pickled Cauliflower

This is a sort of summer salad pickle which can be kept in the refrigerator for several weeks and used as a salad alone or with a garnish. It should be made with Florence fennel but if this is not available 1 teaspoon of fennel seeds will give the flavour if not the texture.

1 medium cauliflower
1 Florence fennel bulb or 1 teaspoon fennel seed
4 stalks celery
2 cloves garlic
1 bay leaf
3 sprigs thyme
juice of 4 medium sized lemons
1 teaspoon salt
½–1 teaspoon black peppercorns

1 cup olive or sesame oil
2 cups water

Break the cauliflower into florets and slice the fennel and celery into small chunks. Combine all ingredients in a saucepan, bring to the boil and simmer for 5 minutes. Allow to cool before storing in jars in the refrigerator at least a day before serving. Garnish to taste with olives, tomato slices, cucumber slices and/or chopped herbs such as parsley or mint.

Pickled Walnuts

Where we live walnuts do not grow so well because of the warm winters. However the Japanese walnut (*Juglans ailantifolia*) does well and although the nuts are small they are good for pickling. The most important things to remember when pickling walnuts are to do it before the shell begins to harden and to protect your hands from the dark brown stain by wearing rubber gloves.

green walnuts
brine
spiced vinegar

Pick the walnuts from the tree when they are large but still soft-shelled — early December is the best time where we live. Wipe the sticky green skin and prick each one 2-3 times with a large needle, rejecting any that are already forming a hard shell under the green skin. Put them in a basin and cover with brine made of 50 g plain salt to every 2½ cups of water. Leave soaking for 7 days. Then drain and discard the brine, cover walnuts with fresh brine and soak another 14 days. Then drain again, wash and dry the nuts and spread out on greaseproof or brown paper exposed to the air so that the walnuts blacken. Do not put them on a good plate or tray because they may stain it. When they are black all over pack them into jars and cover with hot spiced vinegar. Seal with plastic lids when cold and keep in a cool dark cupboard. They are ready to eat in about a month and are delicious with cold meats or cheese.

SAUCES

Horseradish Sauce

My father was very fond of horseradish and grew a bed of it. He dug it in autumn and mother and I took turns to mince it with the tears streaming from our eyes. Perhaps the inventor of the blender had a father who grew horseradish! It is such a pungent herb that it still makes me cry as I prepare it but the tears are worth it for the flavour.

Dig fat roots of horseradish when the plant dies back in autumn/early winter. Cut the top 5 cm off the roots and replant as root cuttings. Put the rest in a basin of cold water, scrub to remove any earth and cut out any blemishes. Do not scrape or peel the roots because the flavour is close to the skin. Slice or chop them quickly, put them in the blender with lemon juice and whizz until the texture is right. If there is no blender cut them in pieces and put through a mincer (and cry). Horseradish loses its flavour when exposed to the air so must be immediately covered with lemon juice or vinegar and then it can be kept in a jar in the refrigerator for future use.

To make the sauce remove 1 tablespoon or more from the jar, squeeze out most of the lemon juice or vinegar and mix it with 1 tablespoon of cream or top milk. Never replace leftover mixed sauce in the jar or the whole lot may turn sour — only take out what you need. Use with hot or cold beef, in sandwiches and with beetroot salads.

Tomato Sauce

This must be the most popular everyday sauce in the western world. It satisfies our need for sweet-sour flavours and is many people's choice for seasoning everything from sausages to stew. Home-made tomato sauce may not be the same vivid red as bought sauce but it does have a lovely flavour.

4.5 *kg tomatoes*
1.5 *kg apples*
1 *kg onions*
500 *g sugar*
2-4 *tablespoons salt to taste*
1 *litre vinegar*
1 *teaspoon whole cloves*
1 *teaspoon whole allspice*
1 *teaspoon blade mace*
1 *teaspoon whole peppercorns*

Chop up the tomatoes, apples and peeled onions and put in a pan. Bring to the boil, stirring, and cook until soft, then rub the pulp through a sieve. Discard tomato skins etc. and return pulp to the pan with spices tied in muslin and the remaining ingredients. Stir well to dissolve the sugar and cook and stir until the sauce is thick enough. I always bottle this in small preserving jars and seal.

There is no love sincerer than the love of food.
G. B. Shaw

Spicy Apple Sauce

Apple sauce is a pleasant alternative to tomato sauce, especially with pork dishes and ham. It is also very nice with any cold meat dishes or it can be added by the tablespoonful to casseroles or soups. Any good-flavoured apple that pulps well may be used. I generally use a cooking apple.

3 kg apples
2 kg onions
2 tablespoons cloves
25 g root ginger
2 teaspoons peppercorns
1 bay leaf
3 sprigs thyme
3 litres vinegar
4 tablespoons salt
4 cups sugar

Chop up the peeled, cored apples and slice peeled onions finely. Put the cloves, ginger and peppercorns in a muslin bag and combine all ingredients in a large preserving pan. Bring to the boil, stirring to dissolve the sugar, and then lower the heat and cook gently until the sauce is thick. Remove the muslin spice bag and bottle the sauce in small preserving jars and seal with vacuum seals.

Plum Sauce

Plum sauce is a rich fruity sauce which my mother made. We used it with cold meats and also in meat loaves and shepherd's pie. It can be added as a sort of 'magic ingredient' to all sorts of meats, casseroles and soups to taste.

3 kg plums
1 kg brown sugar
1.5 litres malt vinegar
6 teaspoons salt
50 g whole ginger
3 teaspoons cloves
2 teaspoons allspice
2 teaspoons pepper

Put the plums, sugar and vinegar and the spices tied in muslin in a pan and bring to the boil, stirring to dissolve the sugar. Boil until the plums are quite soft and then strain out the stones. Return the pulp to the pan and cook until the sauce is thick enough. Pour into bottles and cork when cold, or pour boiling into small jars, overflow and seal with rings and seals.

$\mathcal{B}$everages

HOME-MADE FRUIT DRINKS

A large basin or a plastic bucket, a jug, a clean teatowel or piece of muslin to cover the container, a funnel and some screw-topped bottles are all that is needed to make non-alcoholic fruit drinks and punches at home. If you have plenty of spare fruit, refreshing still and sparkling drinks are so easy to make and are delicious and economical. Certain drinks seem to become family favourites and children quickly learn to make them. If the bottles are washed out properly as soon as they are empty and stacked upside down in boxes to dry, they can be recycled many times and are always to hand for the next brew.

Blackcurrant Syrup

When the children were small I used to make this as a pleasant way for them to take vitamin C. We always called it Beetles' Blood!

1.5 kg blackcurrants
3 litres water
sugar

Wash the currants and cook them gently in a pan with the water until soft. Then mash them to extract the juice and strain through muslin in a sieve. Measure the liquid and add ¾ cup sugar to every cup of juice. Bring to the boil, stirring to dissolve the sugar. Boil 5 minutes then pour into warmed, dried jars, overflow and seal.

Dilute to taste — about ½ cup syrup to 2½-3 cups of water — and drink either hot or cold.

Lemon Water

Of all flavours I find lemon the most refreshing and when added to water it encourages us to drink more of 'Adam's ale', which is a very healthy habit. On the whole people don't drink enough water — instead they drink coffee, tea, fruit juices and alcohol. However water is the true thirst quencher and drinking 6-8 cups of it a day is beneficial. If you don't like the taste of water, lemon water is the answer.

Slice a whole Lisbon lemon into a large jug and fill it up with water. Stand it in a cool place or in the refrigerator for 30 minutes and drink as much as you want. Don't drink it ice cold, just pleasantly cool. Top up the jug with water until all the lemon flavour disappears and then make a fresh lot with a new lemon.

Rhubarb Punch

This is a pleasant early spring drink made by my friend Jean Dickson. The flavours of rhubarb and citrus fruits combine well and make it very refreshing. Decorated with borage flowers and mint leaves or slices of orange or lemon it is a lovely punch for any party.

1 kg rhubarb
1 litre water
1½ cups sugar
1 cup orange juice
¼ cup lemon juice
small bottle of lemonade
borage flowers, mint leaves, or lemon/orange slices

Boil the rhubarb in the water until soft and strain through muslin. Heat the liquid again, stir in the sugar and bring to the boil. Remove from the heat and leave to cool. Then add citrus juices. Just before serving add lemonade and borage flowers etc.

Lemon Beer

Why this drink is called beer I don't know. It has no hops or alcohol in it and is a recipe my mother used to make all summer. Keep it in the refrigerator in screw-topped preserving jars. It can be made with any lemons but I prefer the flavour of Lisbon lemons. The same recipe can be used for limes and/or lemonades.

2 lemons
4 litres boiling water
½-1 cup sugar

Slice the lemons into a basin. Cover with the boiling water, stir in the sugar and allow to cool. Then squeeze the juice out of the lemon slices, strain the liquid into jars and store in the refrigerator. Drink undiluted. If you have a thirsty family make it in the evening and it will be ready for the next day.

Iced Tea

Many farmers and shepherds going out for the day on horseback used to carry a bottle or two of cold tea, strained from the breakfast teapot, in the saddlebag. This is a refreshing variation.

2 lemons
2 cups sugar
2 teaspoons China or Indian tea
1 litre boiling water

Peel the lemon rind thinly into a basin and add the sugar and tea. Pour on the boiling water, stir, cover and allow to cool. Pour into a jug when cold and add lemon juice. Chill before serving.

Lemon Champagne

This is a delicious fizzy lemon drink that must be bottled in screw-topped containers so that the fizz can be controlled as the bottles are opened. It is very disappointing to have most of the liquid on the ceiling and only half a glassful left in the bottle! If you have difficulties with it, reduce the quantity of raisins.

6-8 lemons (depending on size)
1 cup raisins
2 kg sugar
1 litre boiling water
15 litres cold water

Slice the lemons into a large container, add the raisins and sugar and stir in the boiling water. When the sugar is dissolved, add cold water and mix well. Cover and leave 4 days. Strain, bottle and cap. Leave 1-2 weeks before using and remember to open carefully.

Orange Syrup

Home-made orange drinks can be wishy-washy but this Victorian recipe combines both sweet and Seville orange flavours with the juice of a lemon and, if you can find it, a tablespoon or two of orange flower water. It is delicious poured over ice-blocks in a glass.

6 large or 8-10 small oranges
1 Seville orange
1.5 litres water
250 g sugar
orange flower water
1 lemon

Use a vegetable peeler to remove the rind of all the oranges without the pith. Put it in a saucepan with 1 litre of cold water and bring just to simmering point for 3-5 minutes — if it boils it will be bitter. In another saucepan dissolve the sugar in 2½ cups of water and boil for 3 minutes. Cool both mixtures and strain into a jug, adding the strained juice of all the oranges plus the lemon juice and orange flower water to taste. Serve chilled or over ice.

Lemonade may be made in the same way, using Lisbon lemons only, with sugar and water.

Grapefruit and Rosemary Punch

When grapefruit ripens there are great quantities of fruit and this drink is a pleasant alternative to grapefruit, orange and lemon syrups. The honey and rosemary soften the somewhat sharp flavour of the grapefruit. Ginger ale may be added to taste if a sparkling drink is wanted.

3-4 sprigs rosemary
1 tablespoon honey or 3 tablespoons sugar
1 cup boiling water
2½-3 cups grapefruit juice
ice cubes

Infuse the rosemary and honey or sugar in boiling water. Cover and allow to cool. When cold, strain into grapefruit juice and serve in glasses half full of ice-blocks.

Rose Champagne

This is a light, fizzy, non-alcoholic treat. It has a distinctive rose flavour and should be drunk lightly chilled. Anyone with fragrant rose bushes can make it but it builds up quite a fizz after a few weeks and needs to be opened carefully. Screw-topped bottles are therefore better than capped bottles because some pressure can be released gradually and this saves the drink being wasted on the ceiling.

8 litres cold boiled water
1.5 kg sugar
4 sliced lemons
4 tablespoons white wine vinegar
2 cups fragrant rose petals

Pour the water over the sugar in a large bucket and stir to dissolve it. Add the sliced lemons, white wine vinegar and rose petals. Mix and leave 24 hours. Squeeze out the lemon juice and squeeze liquid from the petals. Strain the liquid into bottles and screw on the tops. Keep 2-3 weeks before use.

Sparkling Fruit Drink

This recipe is suitable for all sorts of fruits except tamarillos. I usually make it with apples but it can taste a bit mild unless a strong-flavoured apple is used. A mixture of fruit such as apple and feijoa can be used too.

1 kg fruit, chopped up but not peeled
750 g sugar
4 litres water
2 sliced lemons
1½ tablespoons white wine or cider vinegar

Combine all the ingredients in a large basin or bucket, stir well to dissolve the sugar and leave, covered with a cloth, for 48 hours. Strain out the fruit, bottle and cap the liquid. Store for 2 weeks before drinking. Screw-topped bottles are best so that some fizz can be let out gently.

Elderflower Champagne

As soon as there are seven flowerheads on the elder trees we begin to make our favourite summer drink. It is light and fizzy with a delicate refreshing flavour, just like the beautiful lacey flowers that are used to make it. Our trees begin to bloom in October and continue on until early February but after Christmas we stop picking the flowers to let berries set for wine and elderberry and blackberry jam — if the birds leave us any.

4 litres boiling water
2½ cups sugar
7 heads of elderflowers
2 sliced lemons
2 tablespoons white wine vinegar

Pour the boiling water over the sugar in a large bucket, stir well and leave to cool. When cold add the remaining ingredients, stir again and leave 24 hours. Then strain through a fine strainer, bottle and cap. Do not fill the bottles too full as this drink is very fizzy. Ready in 1-2 weeks.

Minted Grapefruit Juice

Anyone with a grapefruit tree has an abundance of fruit for making this drink which can be made with any type of grapefruit including wheeny grapefruit. It is a delicious drink any time of day. The amount of sugar can be varied to taste but always use some because it helps bring out the flavour of the mint.

1 cup water
¼–½ cup sugar
½ cup chopped mint leaves
6 cups strained fresh grapefruit juice
mint sprigs to garnish

Combine water and sugar in a saucepan, stirring to dissolve the sugar. Add the mint and simmer for 5 minutes. Remove from heat, cover the saucepan and allow to steep for 20 minutes. Strain the mint syrup into a jug, add the grapefruit juice and chill, covered, for at least an hour. Serve garnished with fresh mint.

A man hath no better thing under the sun
to eat, and to drink and to be merry.
Ecclesiasties 8:15

Elderflower Champagne

WINE

Making wine is a lot of fun and as long as consuming alcohol does not become an absorbing hobby the whole family can enjoy it. When I was small we made ginger beer with a 'bug' and regulating the fizz became quite an art. With so many windfall apples cider was inevitable and feijoa wine too. Then we became involved in wine grapes, so now there is something brewing and bubbling most of the year. Now the pre-dinner drink is very often home-made and, if there should be a failure, it generally makes good vinegar!

Equipment

Most of the equipment needed will already be in the house but there are also specialist brewers' supply shops which stock everything.

We use:

1. Large basins, plastic buckets or rubbish bins or wooden barrels for mixing fruit and water, and a wooden spoon.

2. Jelly bags or muslin for straining or covering.

3. A measuring jug, a funnel, a length of plastic or rubber tube for siphoning.

4. 2 litre glass jars for fermenting.

5. Air locks or cotton wool to keep insects out and allow air to escape.

6. Bottles and corks or caps for the final product.

Sometimes the fruit and water need to be heated and the preserving pan or a large saucepan can be used but *never* use a metal container to ferment the wine and *always* make sure all the equipment is scrupulously clean. The easiest way to sterilise bottles, buckets, etc. after washing them out is to dissolve 100 g sodium meta-bisulphite (from the chemist or the brewers' supply shop) in 2 litres of cold water. Rinse the equipment clean with this, drain the solution back into

a bottle, keep it tightly corked and it may be used time and time again.

Most wines are made simply from fruit or flowers, sugar and wine yeast. Sometimes tannin in the form of cold tea is added. The juice of an orange or lemon and, in cases where the fruit contains a lot of pectin, a pectin enzyme, will help to clear the wine. Do not use bakers' or brewers' yeast. Proper wine yeasts are available from brewers' supply shops and should be used according to the directions on the packet.

Try not to leave a big airspace on top of the wine in the fermentation bottles because wine can turn vinegary with exposure to air.

Red Wine

There is something very special about the grape harvest — the vendage — the weather is always hot and still and the fat bunches of purple fruit fill the boxes quickly as we move up the rows cutting the stems. The dew is heavy in the mornings and the Tintara leaves are already glowing with autumn red. We work late because the fruit must be stripped and weighed as soon as possible. At the end of the day we fall into bed and sleep soundly.

To every 3-4 kg black wine grapes add 4 litres cold water and 1.5 kg sugar.

Strip the grapes from their stalks and weigh them into a bucket or bin. Squash them with your hands or put plastic bags on your feet and tread them. Do not crush them so hard that the pips are broken or the flavour of the wine will be spoilt. Cover the fruit with the cold water, stir in 500 g sugar and cover the container with a cloth. Leave for 7 days, stirring the mixture each day. If the colour is rich enough, strain the grapes out through muslin and press out as much juice as possible. I have a small wooden press and after the grapes are strained out through muslin, I put them in the press to get every last drop of juice. Add the rest of the sugar, stir the wine well and use a plastic jug and a funnel to fill 2 litre glass flagons with the liquid. Fit air locks on the flagons or top them with cotton wool and leave the wine to ferment. When bubbles cease to rise, siphon the wine into clean bottles and cork it. Leave it at least 6 months to mature before drinking.

White Wine

White wine is made in much the same way as red wine but our white grapes ripen later, becoming almost golden on the vines. Fortunately the birds are not so interested in the white grapes and, although we have only a few vines, we manage to harvest most of the fruit.

> 2 *kg white wine grapes*
> 4 *litres hot, boiled water*
> 1-1.25 *kg sugar*

Strip the grapes from their stems and crush them as for red wine in a bucket or bin. Cover with hot water which has been boiled and then allowed to cool a little. Cover the container with a cloth and leave 4-5 days, stirring every day. Strain the fruit out through a sieve, press all the juice out and discard the fruit. Add the sugar and stir until it is dissolved in the liquid. Pour this into flagons, fit with air locks and leave to ferment until the bubbles cease to rise. Siphon into dry bottles, cork and leave 6 months to mature.

Feijoa Wine

Like apples, feijoas seem to produce great quantities of fruit and one way of using the surplus is to make wine. Feijoa wine is very nice as long as it is kept a while before it is drunk. An old feijoa wine is much better than a young one. Personally I find the flavour of the fruit skins overpowering and I always scoop the fruit out or peel it.

To each 4 litres of water add:

> 1.5 *kg feijoas*
> 1 *kg sugar*
> 50 *g raisins*
> 1 *teaspoon wine yeast dissolved in* 1½ *cups water at blood heat*

Peel or scoop out the feijoas. Dissolve the sugar in 1 litre boiling water in a large container, add the remaining water and cool. When the yeast is frothy add that. Cover the container with a cloth and leave to work 1-2 weeks. Do not allow the fruit to become mushy. If it does, strain it out sooner. Strain out the fruit, add the raisins and pour into glass bottles or plastic containers fitted with airlocks. Allow to ferment until the wine stops working. Siphon off into clean bottles, straining out the raisins, and leave 6-12 months before drinking. If the wine settles, siphon it again. The flavour of the wine is warm and fruity — its effects can be quite powerful.

Passionfruit Wine

Passionfruit love to grow against a sunny shed wall where their roots can get in underneath and the vine can grow up high. Such a vine can crop well for years. The wine is very full flavoured but light coloured. More colour can be given by chopping the skins and adding them to the pulp.

48 *passionfruit*
4 *litres cold water*
1.75 *kg sugar*

Scoop the pulp out of the passionfruit into a bucket and add the water. Leave 48 hours, then strain the pulp out and stir in the sugar. Pour into flagons and leave to ferment with a small plug of cotton wool in the top of each jar to allow the air to escape. Leave to work for 1-3 weeks depending on fermentation, then siphon into clean bottles and cork or cap them. Store in a cool place for 6 months before drinking.

Elderberry Wine

In some places elderberries can be gathered wild if the berries can be saved from the birds. I find it quite a race as the birds get up first! However, the wine is delicious and worth the effort. High clusters can often be reached by pulling them down with the handle of a walking stick or umbrella.

1.5 *kg elderberries*
1.5 *kg sugar*
4 *litres water*
wine yeast and nutrient

Strip the berries from their stalks with a fork and weigh them into a plastic bucket with half the sugar. Pour on boiling water, stir well and leave to cool before adding wine yeast and nutrient. Keep the wine covered but stir daily for 3 days. Then strain the wine onto the remaining sugar and stir to dissolve it. Pour the mixture into dark glass containers and allow it to ferment. When bubbles cease to rise, siphon into clean bottles and cork. Leave 6 months before drinking.

Woodruff Wine

Sweet woodruff (*Galium odoratum*) is a low-growing, bright green, shade-loving herb with leaves arranged in whirls around the stems. It is a cousin of that weed herb that sticks to skin and clothes known as cleavers or goosegrass. Woodruff has no smell when it is fresh but once dried it has the sweet scent of new-mown hay. It is used to flavour dry white wine and in that beautiful punch known as Maibowle.

2-3 *sprigs dried woodruff*
1 *bottle dry white wine*
1 *bottle champagne or lemonade or similar fizz*
borage flowers and strawberries

Pick the woodruff and allow it to dry in a shady place for 2-3 days. Then add it to a bottle of dry white wine, cork the bottle and chill for several hours in the refrigerator. If you want a totally alcoholic punch, combine in the punch bowl with a bottle of champagne. If everyone has to drive home use a bottle of fizzy lemonade instead. Decorate with borage flowers and small strawberries.

Dandelion Wine

Of all 'weeds' dandelion is the most useful: the leaves are good both raw and cooked, the roots make a caffeine-free coffee and the flowers are used for wine. I cultivate a patch and they are naturalised in the orchard.

2 *litres dandelion flowers*
4 *litres boiling water*
1 *lemon*
1 *orange*
1.5 *kg sugar*
wine yeast

Pick dandelion flowers using a measuring jug or similar to calculate required volume, and tip them into a bucket. Add the boiling water and the sliced fruit and leave them to steep for 5 days. Keep covered with a cloth. Strain the flowers and fruit out and pour the liquid onto the sugar. Stir well to dissolve. Add the yeast, pour into jars fitted with airlocks and leave until the wine stops fermenting. Siphon off into clean bottles and cork or cap. Leave 6 months before drinking.

Spiced Plum Wine

Plums make a rich, red and heady wine and this recipe gives a warming drink for wet winter days. Any plums can be used and a few stones left in improve the flavour. Keep 6 months before drinking.

2 kg plums
25 g root ginger
6 cloves
1 orange
1 lemon
4 litres boiling water
wine yeast
2 kg sugar

Slice the plums and discard most of the stones. Put the fruit into a large bucket with the spices and sliced orange and lemon. Pour on boiling water, mashing the fruit, and leave to cool before adding the wine yeast. Cover the container with a cloth and stir daily for 5 days. Strain the liquid onto the sugar, discard the fruit, and stir well. Pour into fermentation jars, fit airlocks and leave until the bubbles cease. Siphon into clear bottles and cork.

Cider

Apple cider is properly made by crushing the juice out of a mixture of sweet, sour and bitter apples. If you have no press, you can finely chop the apples or mince them, or blend them with some water. I recently blended some apples and water for cider but found that the amount of pectin had made the liquid very cloudy. The clearest cider we make is by chopping the apples, although it is the slowest method.

any quantity of apples
boiling water to cover
1 cup sugar to every 4 litres liquid

Chop up whole apples, including skins, pips and cores — windfalls will do — and cover with boiling water in a wooden tub or plastic bin. Do not fill the tub or bin too full, otherwise, when the mixture ferments and expands, the liquid will overflow. Cover the container with a cloth and leave it to stand for 3-4 days, stirring every day. Then crush the apples as much as possible and strain the liquid through a jelly bag into a plastic bucket.

Add 1 cup of sugar to every 4 litres of the juice. Stir well to dissolve the sugar and pour into 2 litre flagons to ferment. Fill the jars nearly to the top and bung with cotton wool or screw on caps lightly, in order to keep insects out but allow gas to escape. Leave until fermentation ceases, then siphon the cider into clean dry bottles and cap. Ready to drink in 2 weeks but better if kept longer.

Cider may be drunk cold or mulled in winter — make a syrup of 1-2 tablespoons of sugar or honey to 1 cup of water. Bring to the boil and add 3 cloves, 5 cm of cinnamon quill and ½ sliced lemon. Simmer 5 minutes. Add 1-2 cups cider and reheat but do not boil.

FRUIT LIQUEURS AND SPIRITS

Brandy, gin and vodka can all be flavoured with fruit. The fruit must be perfect and perfectly ripe and usually some castor sugar or sugar syrup is necessary. Soft fruit such as strawberries, raspberries, blackberries, mulberries, blackcurrants and cherries are all suitable. Fill a preserving jar with perfect fruit, add castor sugar to about one-third of the way up the jar and then fill it with brandy, gin or vodka.

With firm fruit such as peaches, pears, quinces and apricots slice or halve the fruit and leave the pips or crack the stones and add the kernels. Make a sugar syrup of 2 cups sugar to 1 cup water, bring it to the boil, stirring to dissolve the sugar, and then simmer for 5 minutes. Cool the syrup. Put the fruit in a preserving jar, add the cold syrup to fill one-third of the jar and top up with brandy, gin or vodka. Leave at least 4 weeks then filter out the fruit and pour the liqueur into clean bottles. If the taste is too sweet pour some liqueur out and top up with spirits without adding any sugar until it tastes right for you. The fruit may be added to trifles etc. if it has a nice flavour, otherwise drain it and discard it. Do *not* feed it to the hens! Spices and orange or lemon peel can be added to liqueurs, to taste.

Damson Gin

This is a simple but potent brew. Fill a glass preserving jar with fat, unblemished damsons and fill the jar also with gin. Cover with a screw-topped lid and leave at the back of the cupboard for 6-12 months. The damsons become even plumper and are a good, quick pick-me-up and the gin can be drunk as a liqueur or diluted to make a long drink with soda and ice. If you prefer, add castor sugar. Fill the jar first with damsons, add castor sugar to about one-third of the way up the jar and then top up with gin. The sugar will dissolve gradually or you can hurry the process by tipping the jar upside down.

Quince Brandy

For those that like them, nothing equals the flavour of quinces, and this recipe makes a beautiful liqueur. If no brandy is available, gin or vodka will do, although, of course, the flavour will be slightly different.

2 ripe quinces
50 g sugar
brandy to cover (or gin or vodka)

Grate the whole quinces, including the skin too, into a large preserving jar. Add the sugar and cover all with brandy. Screw on a plastic lid and leave the jar in a cupboard for 8 weeks. Strain out the pulp and taste the liqueur — add more sugar if necessary. The pulp may be kept in a jar for a short time and added to other fruit desserts in small quantities.

A full cupboard bespeaketh a generous heart.
Anon

Preserving

My father was very fond of fruit and it was a major part of our diet. We ate grapefruit for breakfast, when it was in season, and the rest of the year we had stewed or bottled fruit with cereal or porridge. There was always fresh fruit for lunch, and my mother made some sort of fruit pudding as part of dinner in the evening. Bananas and oranges were the only fruits bought, though sometimes we had tinned pineapple for a treat, otherwise Dad grew it all.

Our home orchard consisted of, at first, four eating apples and a beautiful cooker, one tree each of grapefruit (a Poorman's Orange), a Meyer lemon, nectarine, quince and pear, two peach trees, three plums and two feijoas. Dad also grew gooseberries, passionfruit, red currants, strawberries and kiwifruit, then known as Chinese gooseberry.

A fair amount of swapping buckets of fruit went on with neighbours and friends, and what could not be eaten fresh was made into jam or chutney or bottled for the winter — there were no freezers in my childhood.

Many people think bottling is a terrible chore but we always found it quite a sociable activity. Everyone would sit round the kitchen table peeling fruit (and eating the extra-nice ripe bits) and having a good chat. When it was over and the washing-up done, there would be bottles full of fruit cooling on the bench and a satisfied feeling all round.

Apricots, peaches, pears and plums are all suitable for bottling, so are feijoas and quinces, but apples are difficult because they pulp down and are hard to overflow. This problem can be solved by topping each jar up with boiling water from the kettle. As a general rule it is better to use late rather than early fruit because it has had time to develop more flavour and a firmer texture.

Early peaches and plums are ideal for eating fresh or when gently stewed but late varieties such as Golden Queen peaches and George Wilson plums are best for bottling. When school begins early in February serious bottlers get the jars washed, find the preserving pan and prepare for action!

Peaches bottle well if you pay attention to detail. If left on the tree until fully ripe peaches bruise easily and are spoilt by handling, so, to tell if a peach is ripe, don't squeeze the sides, instead gently feel the tip of the fruit and if it is soft the peach is ready to pick. Ripe peaches smell aromatic, too.

Picking is easy — holding the fruit gently but firmly, twist it anti-clockwise and it should separate cleanly from the branch. Place each peach carefully in the bucket, stem-end down to protect the riper tip, and continue until the bucket is full. Never tip the peaches out into a box — transfer them by hand and, if they are not ripe enough to eat or bottle, spread them out on a dish or in a tray in a single, or at most double, layer, still stem end down. If the tips are soft they should be ready in a day or two — if left at room temperature. If they are ripe but you have no time to bottle them immediately, they will keep one to two days in the fridge. If the fruit is affected by brown rot, however, the disease will spread rapidly, even overnight, so cut the bad patches out and peel and cook the fruit as soon as possible.

It is not necessary to totally reject damaged fruit — surface skin blemishes can be peeled off and bird pecks cut out as the fruit is prepared, and good parts of brown rot-infected fruit be sliced off into the pan.

The best peach varieties for bottling are those which ripen from the middle of January onwards. Older types such as Paragon, A1 and Stark — all firm, yellow-fleshed, cling-stone peaches — or Mary's Choice or Kalamazoo — firm, yellow-fleshed, freestone peaches — are good. White Elberta — a sweet white-fleshed freestone — and Blackboy — a beetroot-coloured freestone — are excellent too, if you can find a tree. Golden Queen, a very late peach, was considered to be the best bottling peach but now a newer variety, Tatura Aurora, is recommended. It ripens even later and is less susceptible to brown rot. Also look for J. H. Hale, Floridaprince, Floragold, Coronet, Redhaven, O'Henry and Fairtime.

Apricots are easy to bottle because they are freestone and do not need to be peeled. Simply run a knife round the groove in the fruit, ease it in half and remove the stone. Cook the apricot halves gently in light syrup (*see* page 63) and add a small number of kernels, obtained by splitting the stones, to give the fruit an almondy flavour.

Nectarines are smooth skinned and bottle beautifully, and the smaller, rounder peacharines are good too.

William's Bon Chrétien, sometimes called Bartlett, is both an eating and a bottling pear which ripens early in February. Packham's Triumph and the self-fertile Keiffer are later and also bottle well. Other varieties are usually eaten raw, and the late season pears, Winter Cole and Winter Nelis, are stored for eating during the winter. These European pears should not be confused with the Asian or Nashi pears.

Pears are always picked firm because they are impossible to handle without bruising when ripe, and they turn brown and soft in the centre if left too long on the tree. To tell if pears are ready to pick consider the size and plumpness of the fruit and its colour — as they ripen the pears' skin becomes a lighter shade of green-brown. Windfalls which soften quickly are another sign the crop is ripe. If ready to pick, the fruit should come away from the branch with stem intact when it is lifted and twisted.

Although Keiffer is self-fertile, most pears crop better if they are planted close to other pear varieties that flower at the same time, so cross pollination can take place. Pears can also be slow to fruit: an old saying has it that you 'plant pears for your heirs'.

Even if they are quite firm when picked, handle pears gently and don't tip them roughly into boxes. It is worthwhile to check through the stored pears every couple of days and sort out ripe fruit for eating or bottling. You will soon learn how to distinguish the ripe fruit, which is delicious, from the over-ripe, which tastes horrid!

Keiffer trees crop well, producing medium-sized brown fruit which are better for cooking than eating. All pear trees seem to grow tall and produce well most seasons.

The best plums for bottling are Doris, Satsuma and George Wilson — the last two are freestone. They can be bottled whole or in halves and do not need to be peeled. However, plums need more sugar than other fruits otherwise they taste quite sharp.

For bottling, fruit is best when ripe but firm. If it is too ripe it goes mushy and often does not taste so good. Peaches and nectarines can be bottled whole, in halves or sliced, but whole fruit does not pack so economically into jars. Freestone peaches can be halved easily and quickly, but clingstone peaches are easier to slice. It is a good idea to keep slices much the same size so they cook evenly, but I always leave a few small peaches whole because the stones give the cooked fruit a nice flavour. I also always peel peaches: when they are ripe the skin comes off more freely.

Pears are generally bottled in halves or quarters. If you find peeling them a slow job, drop the prepared fruit into a basin of cold water to which the juice of a lemon has been added. This will stop the pears turning brown. If they do turn brown they generally come back to white as they cook. I bottle pears with a little honey instead of sugar and add a piece of Lisbon lemon peel to each jar.

Quinces are quite a 'woody' fruit to peel because, even when they are golden on the tree their flesh is still very firm. I generally quarter the fruit and peel and remove the pips before slicing each quarter into 2-4 pieces. Then the slices cook more quickly. When tender, the quince slices should be bottled like pears.

If the quince peelings are tied in muslin and cooked in the syrup with the fruit they will give it a good pink colour.

Both late-season eating–apples — like Golden Delicious and Granny Smith — and cooking apples — like Ballarat — may be sliced, cooked in light syrup and bottled. However, because they pulp down, air is sometimes trapped in the fruit which sinks down in the bottles as it cools. This may prevent the jars sealing, or allow mould to grow on the top of the fruit as there is too much air surface exposed. It is best to top up all apples with boiling water from a simmering kettle, to overflow each jar before sealing.

Feijoas bottle well either peeled whole or cut in half and the pulp scooped out. Do not boil too vigorously or the fruit becomes rather mushy.

Tamarillos can be skinned like tomatoes by putting them in a basin and covering them with boiling water for 5 minutes. Then pour the water off. The skins should peel off easily with a sharp knife and the fruit can then be cooked either sliced or whole and bottled.

Kiwifruit can also be bottled whole but wash the peeled fruit to remove any brown hairs (as they do not improve the taste!) before cooking.

Combinations such as blackberries and apples or peaches, pears and passionfruit, also bottle well together. When using passionfruit, though, scoop the pulp out, heat this in a separate saucepan and pour the desired amount into the jar to be topped up with other fruit. In this way any pips are less likely to reach the top and prevent the lid sealing when the jar is overflowed.

EQUIPMENT

1. A large preserving pan and a long-handled wooden spoon.

2. Agee or other suitable jars with screw bands and seals.

3. A plastic jug for filling jars.

4. A frying pan to stand the jars in to save syrup spilling everywhere.

5. A cloth to lift hot jars with, to avoid burning yourself.

6. Folded newspaper or a wooden board to stand jars on to cool — they may crack if set down on a cool bench top.

Syrup

Fruit can be bottled in water but sugar brings out the flavour of fruit and helps keep it a good colour, so generally fruit is bottled in a syrup made with white, brown or raw sugar or honey.

This can be made to taste — a medium syrup is made by combining ½-1 cup sugar and 2 cups water, stirred together in a preserving pan until the sugar is dissolved. Then bring it to the boil and boil for 1-2 minutes before adding the prepared fruit. You will need

approximately 1½–2 cups syrup to every 1–litre jar, depending on whether the fruit is sliced or left whole. 4 kg peaches or pears, sliced, will fill 3 or 4 1–litre jars and 4 kg plums will fill 4 or 5 1–litre jars. More jars with less fruit in each jar result if the peaches are bottled whole.

Successful bottling by the overflow method depends on speed and efficiency, so get everything ready beforehand.

Because you will be working with boiling-hot fruit and syrup, make sure there are no small children close and that floor and bench spaces are clear, to prevent accidents.

While the fruit is coming to the boil in the preserving pan I put 4 to 6 clean 1–litre jars to soak in hot water in the sink (always check the jars and don't use any that are cracked or chipped). As well, check that the screw bands fit the jars and have a seal ready for each band.

Fill the frying pan with hot water to warm it up so the jars don't crack when you stand them in it.

Put a board or folded newspaper on the bench ready for the hot jars, and have a cloth ready to lift them on to the board.

When the fruit is cooked, tip the water out of the frying pan and put it on the bench close to the preserving pan. Tip the water out of the first jar and dry it with a clean dry tea towel. Stand the jar in the frying pan and use the plastic jug to fill it with boiling fruit and syrup, topping up the jar with extra syrup so it overflows. Cover immediately with the seal and screw on the band. Lift the jar out of the pan on to the board using a cloth. Then wipe the sides of the jar clean with the dish cloth.

Tip the syrup from the frying pan back into the preserving pan, bring it to the boil again, take the next jar out of hot water and dry it and fill it as before. Continue until all the fruit is bottled. As the jars cool the seals should 'pop' and dip down.

When the jars are cold remove the screw bands, wipe around the top of the jars and store them in a cool dry cupboard.

If the seal does not sink inwards, the jar is not sealed properly and the fruit will not keep. Usually this is caused by either the fruit and syrup not being hot enough when the jar was filled — it must be boiling — or the seal was not put on quickly enough, or air was trapped in the jar which rose to the surface and left a gap between the top of the fruit and the seal. Sometimes a small piece of fruit gets caught under the seal around the edge of the jar and stops it sealing properly.

If the jar is not sealed, take off the lid, tip the fruit back into the pan, bring it to the boil and overflow and seal it as before using a fresh seal — seals cannot be re-used but of course jars and screw bands can be used many times.

Preserving jars, screw bands and seals are usually available in supermarkets.

For pears I use 1 tablespoon of honey to each jar, made into syrup with water, and add some thinly peeled Lisbon lemon rind as well. Peaches and pears can be bottled together too. Bottled fruit can be used like stewed fruit or for pie fillings, crumbles, sponge puddings, etc., though the syrup should be drained out first and can be used with muesli or in jellies.

Bottled fruit is a marvellous standby, only needing to be opened and tipped into a dish to be ready to eat. Fresh fruit may be best, but bottled fruit is delicious and an economical way to enjoy summer fruits in winter.

Do *not* use the overflow method to bottle vegetables, meat or fish.

Pumpkin pie

Scones, Cakes Puddings, & NIBBLES

Hazelnut Loaf

This is a recipe from some German friends who made it for us once as a parting present. I think of them every time I make it, especially as I arrange the nuts on top. It is a lovely way to remember someone.

150 g butter
150 g sugar
1 teaspoon vanilla
2 eggs
125 g minced hazelnuts
200 g flour
2 teaspoons baking powder
milk

Icing:
1-2 tablespoons water, lemon juice or rum
125 g icing sugar
whole hazelnuts for decoration

Cream the butter and sugar in a bowl until light and fluffy. Beat in the vanilla, beaten egg and finely chopped or minced hazelnuts. Sift in the flour and baking powder and add just enough milk to allow the dough to drip off the spoon in lumps. Bake in a greased loaf tin at 175°C for 40-45 minutes. Turn out and cool on a rack. When cold, ice with icing made by adding 1-2 tablespoons of liquid to the sifted icing sugar and make a pattern with whole hazelnuts along the loaf.

Orange and Lemon Buns

This is a sweet bun recipe using both orange and lemon rind. Grating citrus rind is a dangerous occupation, and I find a zester is a very useful gadget, giving thin strips of peel with no pith very quickly and easily. It is also much easier to clean than a grater.

50 g butter
¼ cup sugar
grated rind 1 orange and 1 lemon
1 egg
2 cups flour
2 teaspoons baking powder
pinch salt
¼ cup orange juice

Cream butter and sugar with citrus zest and beat in beaten egg. Add sifted flour, baking powder and salt alternately with orange juice. Add a little milk if necessary to make a soft dough. Knead lightly on a floured surface, roll out 2 cm thick and cut into 5 cm diameter rounds. Place these close together on a greased baking tray and cook for 15 minutes at 210°C.

Feijoa Scones

These scones are sweet in much the same way as date scones, so are really best eaten as is, or with a little butter. They are nice for afternoon or morning teas and those 'ladies-a-plate' situations.

2 cups flour
2 teaspoons baking powder
50 g butter
¼ cup sugar (or to taste)
¾ cup chopped raw feijoas
1 egg
milk to mix

Sift together flour and baking powder and rub in chopped butter until the mixture resembles breadcrumbs. Add sugar to taste depending on the ripeness/sweetness of the fruit, then stir in peeled chopped feijoas. Beat the egg and add with sufficient milk to make a soft dough. Knead quickly and lightly on a floured surface and roll out about 1 cm thick. Cut into 5 cm rounds with a floured glass or pastry cutter and then place rounds close together on a greased tray. Bake for about 15 minutes at 210°C.

Courgette or Zucchini Loaves

In a good season a couple of plants produce so many courgettes that it is almost impossible to keep up with them. However everyone loves these loaves and if a few courgettes grow too large to eat I grate them into 2-cup lots and store them in the deep freeze for winter baking.

3 eggs
2 cups raw sugar
3 teaspoons vanilla essence
1 cup safflower oil
2 cups grated courgette

3 cups flour
1 teaspoon salt
1 teaspoon baking soda
3 teaspoons cinnamon
1 cup walnuts

Use an electric beater to beat the eggs in a large bowl until light and fluffy. Then beat in the sugar, vanilla and oil until the mixture is smooth. Drain the mixture from the beaters into the bowl and stir in the courgettes. Sift together the flour, salt, soda and cinnamon and fold in alternately with the chopped walnuts. Pour the mixture into two 22 x 10 cm loaf tins and bake at 180°C for about an hour. Cool on a wire rack.

Pumpkin and Orange Loaf

The texture of pumpkin makes a good loaf, and cooked mashed pumpkin can also be used in scones and cakes. This recipe makes a nice change from pumpkin pie and the zest of the orange gives a delicious flavour.

200 g pumpkin
½ cup brown sugar
6 tablespoons milk
2 tablespoons butter
zest of 1 orange
½ cup walnuts or almonds
½ cup sultanas
2 eggs
2 cups wholemeal flour
2 teaspoons baking powder

Cook the peeled pumpkin until tender, then drain in a sieve and cool. Mix the sugar with 3 tablespoons of milk in a bowl and beat in the butter and orange zest. Add the nuts and sultanas, mashed pumpkin and eggs beaten with the remaining milk. Fold in the sifted flour and baking powder and mix well. Pour into a greased loaf tin and bake 1 hour at 180°C.

Blueberry Muffins

Blueberries are a relatively new fruit in the southern hemisphere but the good old American recipes have followed them and we, too, can have home-made blueberry muffins that taste really good.

1½ cups fresh or frozen blueberries
1½ cups flour
3 teaspoons baking powder
3 tablespoons sugar
1 egg
¾ cup milk
3 tablespoons melted butter

Wash and drain the blueberries — they should be as dry as possible. Sift the flour and baking powder into a bowl and mix in the sugar. Beat the egg, add the milk and stir into the flour. Then add the blueberries and finally the melted butter. Mix well and pour into greased muffin tins, filling each about three-quarters full. Bake 20 minutes at 200°C and cool on a rack.

Apple Muffins

Muffins are a meal in themselves, excellent for morning or afternoon tea. This recipe may be varied by adding ginger or mixed spice, dried fruit or chopped walnuts. Muffins can be buttered but I like them just as they are.

1 cup bran
¾ cup milk
1 tablespoon golden syrup
1 teaspoon baking soda
1 beaten egg
¾ cup flour
pinch salt
1 cup chopped apple

Soak the first four ingredients for 5 minutes then add the remaining ingredients. Mix well and half-fill greased muffin pans with the mixture. Bake 20 minutes at 180°C.

PUDDINGS

Fruit Pies

The heavenly combination of fruit and pastry seems to be the way to everyone's heart. The smell of apple pie takes me back to the kitchen at the farm and Mrs Tombleson making feather-light pastry with her home-made butter and turnovers with thinly sliced apple, baking tray after tray of them in the hot oven of the Aga stove. Some of the juice from the apples would escape and caramelise round the edges.

A fruit pie is usually made by filling an ovenproof dish nearly full of finely sliced fruit, sprinkling a little sugar, to bring out the flavour, between the layers. A pie funnel should be placed in the middle to hold up the crust and a thin strip of pastry stuck all round the dish should be dampened with a little water so that the pastry top will stick and form a complete cover.

When making pastry it is important to keep all the ingredients cold — old kitchens sometimes had a marble slab in the bench for pastry making. If the cold butter is too hard, it can be grated into the flour but keep your hands cold and knead the dough lightly and quickly. Always let the pastry rest in a cool place for about 30 minutes before rolling it out so it will not shrink when it is cooking.

Apple Pie

50 g butter to every 1 cup flour
cold water
apples
sugar to taste
2-3 cloves

Make the pastry by chopping the butter into the flour in a bowl until it is crumbly. Then add just enough cold water to make a firm dough. Knead it quickly and lightly on a cold floured surface and when it is smooth roll it into a ball. Wrap it in a piece or two of grease-proof or butter paper, and leave to rest in the refrigerator or a cool place for half an hour. While the pastry rests prepare the fruit.

Peel, core and slice the apples into the pie dish, sprinkling a little sugar between layers of fruit arranged around the pie funnel. Fill the dish quite full because the fruit will sink as it cooks. Put the peelings and cores in a small saucepan with 1/2 cup of water, bring it to the boil and simmer a few minutes. Strain the liquid into a bowl and cool it, discarding peel and pips. When cool, add the liquid to the pie and place 2-3 whole cloves among the apples. Roll out the pastry and cut a thin strip to cover the top edge of the pie dish. Dampen it with a little cold water.

Roll out the rest of the pastry and cover the pie completely, pressing the edges down firmly with a fork to make a pattern, and stick the crust to the lining dough. Trim the edges and use the pastry trimmings to decorate the top of the pie. Prick it to allow the steam to escape and bake at 210°C for 15 minutes. Reduce heat to 180°C and cook a further 15 minutes.

A grated quince or a handful or two of blackberries may be used instead of cloves to flavour the pie.

Fig Puddings

Fresh figs are delicious split and eaten straight from the tree — ask any bird! — but cooked fresh figs are also wonderful as long as they are poached or baked in a light syrup flavoured with a vanilla pod or a little lemon peel, green ginger or orange juice, and not overcooked or mushy. They can be set in a casserole, stem ends up, in a little lemon or orange juice, sugar and water, and then cooked gently in a cool oven and served warm or cold with cream and some freshly grated lemon or orange rind.

Poached figs can be flavoured by adding fresh root ginger and lemon rind to the syrup. For an extra special occasion stuff figs carefully with chopped walnuts and 1 teaspoon of honey and heat them gently in a pan with ½-1 cup of port, basting them frequently. Serve them hot with cream.

Apple Dumplings

Coleridge holds that a man cannot have a pure mind who refuses apple dumpling and, for me, the combination of crisp pastry and melting apple spiced with sugar and a clove is the ultimate apple treat.

125 g butter
2 cups flour
cold water to mix
6 small apples
6 teaspoons brown sugar
6 small cloves

Cut the butter into the flour until it is crumbly and mix to a stiff dough with cold water. Knead quickly and allow the pastry to rest in the refrigerator for 30 minutes. Peel and core the apples. Divide the pastry into 6 pieces and roll out each piece into a square. Put an apple on each square and tip a teaspoon of brown sugar into each core cavity. Pop in a clove too and then wrap the pastry neatly round the apple. Use a little milk or water on the underside of the pastry join to seal it. Put the dumplings into a baking dish and bake at 200°C for about 30 minutes. Serve warm with whipped cream.

The apple juice can escape from the pastry so always bake in a dish rather than on an oven tray. Other fillings such as dates, raisins, nuts and spices or lemon peel may be used instead of cloves to stuff the dumplings.

Medlar Tart

This is a variation of an Elizabethan dish and it can be made as an open tart or covered with a crust. I prefer a shortcake-type pastry and stir sugar to taste and either ground ginger, cinnamon or cloves into the medlar pulp. Any citrus peel, grated, can be added and a mixture of apple and medlar pulp (*see* Medlar Jelly p. 28) gives a good flavour. The Elizabethans thickened the pulp with egg yolks but this doesn't seem necessary.

Shortcrust pastry:
50 g butter
1 cup flour
1 tablespoon sugar
1 egg

Rub the butter into the flour until it is crumbly. Add the sugar and knead to a dough with the beaten egg. Roll out on a floured surface and line a tart tin or shallow ovenproof dish. Beat the sugar and spice into the medlar pulp until it tastes right and add the finely grated citrus peel. Fill the tart with this mixture and bake at 180°C for 30 minutes.

Berry Flan

This can be made with any berries — blackberries, blueberries, currants, gooseberries, raspberries or strawberries. Other fruits such as apricots, peaches or cherries would be suitable, too. The fruit must be cooked separately and a flan tin should be used.

¼ cup butter
¼ cup sugar
2 eggs
½ cup flour
½ teaspoon baking powder
1½ cups drained, stewed berries

1 *heaped teaspoon arrowroot*
2 *teaspoons cold water*
1 *cup syrup from berries*

Cream the butter and sugar and mix in the beaten eggs. Fold in the sifted flour and baking powder and pour the mixture into a well greased flan tin. Bake at 190°C for 15-20 minutes. Turn out onto a rack to cool. When cold, fill with drained fruit. Make a glaze by mixing the arrowroot and cold water and stirring in the hot berry syrup. Bring to the boil and cook, stirring for several minutes. Cool slightly and pour over the fruit to glaze it.

Potato and Apple Cake

This is an Irish recipe in which potatoes are used to make a pastry which is then filled with cooking apples. It is a lovely hot dish on a cold day and if there is any left it may be served cold later.

500 g potatoes
25 g butter
1 teaspoon castor sugar
1 cup flour
500 g cooking apples
1 tablespoon butter
2 tablespoons sugar

Peel and slice the potatoes and cook in boiling water until tender. Drain them well and mash, then mix in the butter, sugar and flour. Turn the pastry onto a floured surface and knead until smooth. Divide the mixture and roll out 2 circles, one of 23 cm diameter and the other of 19 cm diameter. Put the smaller circle on a baking tray or in a round, greased pie dish. Cover the potato pastry with sliced apples, leaving a 2 cm margin, and sprinkle with 1 tablespoon of sugar. Dampen the edges and cover with the larger pastry circle. Prick to allow steam to escape and bake at 190° C

until lightly browned (30-40 minutes).

Remove from the oven and, with a sharp pointed knife, cut a small circle out of the top and lift it off carefully. Put the remaining tablespoonfuls of sugar and butter inside and replace the circle. Return to the oven for 5 minutes so the filling mixes. Serve as is or sprinkle with a little raw sugar.

Mandarin and Marmalade Tart

Like baklava, this tart is made with filo pastry but the sharpness and strong flavour of the marmalade give quite a different taste. The unbuttered edges of the filo bake crisp and the poached mandarin slices are plump and juicy, so there is a wonderful contrast of textures. Other citrus can be used in place of mandarins but should always be lightly cooked, not raw.

1¼ cups finely chopped walnuts
½ cup fine breadcrumbs
1 cup marmalade
2 tablespoons orange liqueur
6 tablespoons unsalted butter
10 sheets filo pastry
500 g peeled mandarins poached in a light syrup and cooled

Mix the walnuts and fine dry breadcrumbs together in a basin. Heat ¾ cup marmalade with the liqueur and 2 tablespoons butter in a saucepan, stirring well, then reduce the heat to allow it to stay just warm. Melt the remaining 4 tablespoons of butter in a basin over hot water. For a 20-cm pie tin, trim the filo sheets into 35-cm squares but keep them covered to stop them drying out, as for baklava.

Brush the pie tin with melted butter and press a sheet of filo into it. Brush the bottom and sides to the edge of the tin with melted butter but do not butter the edges above the tin. Layer 3 more sheets of filo in the pie tin in the same way. Then sprinkle a third of the walnut mixture over and cover it with a third of the warmed marmalade. Add 2 more filo sheets brushed with melted butter and cover with one-third each of the walnuts and marmalade, then repeat again. Arrange the edges of the filo in a decorative collar and bake at 190°C for 30-35 minutes in the lower part of the oven. Let the tart cool 10 minutes on a rack, then gently place an empty tin on the centre, turn the tart upside down and remove the pie tin. Invert the tart onto a serving plate and arrange the mandarin slices in a spiral in the centre. Strain the remaining marmalade mixture and brush it over the mandarin. Serve with Turkish coffee.

Dutch Apple or Pear Tart

Dutch fruit tarts both look and taste delicious. They are best made with cooking apples or with equal quantities of cooking apples and pears. The zest of a lemon complements the short pastry and cinnamon and the slivered almonds give a crunchy texture. This is Jeanette's recipe.

225 *g unsalted butter*
100 *g wholemeal flour*
250 *g white flour*
1 *teaspoon baking powder*
150 *g raw sugar*
pinch salt
1 *egg*
6-8 *cooking apples*
50 *g sultanas*
slivered almonds

Cut the butter into the mixed flour, baking powder, sugar and salt and stir in the egg. Knead well and leave the dough for ½ hour in a cool place. Peel, core and slice the apples. Line a 22 cm spring-form tin with greased foil and sprinkle it with breadcrumbs or flour. Roll out the dough and line the foil with half of it. Arrange 2 layers of sliced fruit sprinkled with

cinnamon, the lemon zest and sultanas over the dough. Cut the rest of the dough in 1 cm strips and plait it like a lattice over the fruit. Dampen the ends of the strips with water so they stick firmly to the edge of the dough. Brush the top with a little milk and sprinkle it with slivered almonds. Bake 1-1¼ hours at 180°C until light brown.

Pumpkin Pie

Last year we had an American visitor at Christmas and were astonished to learn that Americans don't have Christmas cake or pudding or crackers or mince pies, but they often have pumpkin pie. So, of course, I had to make one on Boxing Day and the expert voted it a good one.

Pastry:
50 *g butter*
1 *cup flour*
cold water

Filling:
5 *tablespoons sugar*
1 *teaspoon each salt and cinnamon*
½ *teaspoon ginger*
¼ *teaspoon nutmeg*
2 *beaten eggs*
1½ *cups milk*
1½ *cups cooked, mashed pumpkin*

Rub the cold chopped butter into the flour until it resembles breadcrumbs and mix to a dough with cold water. Knead till smooth and rest, covered, in the refrigerator for 30 minutes. Then roll out on a floured surface and use to line a greased 25 cm pie plate.

Make the filling by combining the sugar and spices and stirring in the beaten eggs, milk and cooked, mashed pumpkin. Pour it into the pastry case and bake at 210°C for 30-40 minutes until the pastry is brown and crisp and the filling set. Serve warm or cold with cream.

Cold Lemon Soufflé

The clean lemony taste of this pudding with its creamy texture and light fluffiness makes it the perfect special dessert to round off any dinner. Children love it, and it has the added advantage of being able to be prepared beforehand. I prefer to use Lisbon lemons but it can also be made with limes or a mixture of sweet and bitter oranges.

3 eggs
1 cup castor sugar
2 lemons
2 teaspoons gelatine
4 tablespoons water
1 cup whipped cream
extra cream and nuts to garnish

Separate eggs and beat yolks with sugar in a basin, gradually adding finely grated rind and strained lemon juice. Place the basin over simmering water in a saucepan and continue to whisk the mixture until it is thick and fluffy. Allow the gelatine to swell in cold water, then dissolve it over hot water and when it is entirely melted add it to the egg yolk mixture. Then fold in the cream and stiffly beaten egg whites and turn it all into a dish and leave it to set in the refrigerator.

Just before serving, decorate with a little extra whipped cream and slivered almonds if you wish.

Apple and Other Fruit Crumbles

The three great standbys of the pudding course are the fruit crumble, the fruit sponge and the fruit topped cake. The fruit can be varied or used in different combinations and the toppings or sponge mixtures flavoured with different spices and seeds. They are all immensely popular and round off any meal very nicely.

Peel and slice apples into a deep pie dish to fill it and add a little finely grated lemon rind. In a bowl make the crumble topping by working ½ cup butter into a mixture of ½ cup sugar and 1 cup wholemeal flour until it resembles breadcrumbs. Spread it over the sliced apple and bake at 180°C for 30 minutes. Serve with cream, ice-cream or custard.

Fruit Variations:
Use stewed apple instead of raw apple or a mixture of stewed apple and pears or quinces, or feijoas, or pears and/or quinces alone.

Topping Variations:
Use brown or raw sugar in place of white sugar.
Use white flour or rolled oats in place of wholemeal flour.
Add ground almonds or coconut to the mixture.
Use 1 teaspoon of ginger, coriander, cinnamon, caraway seeds, mixed spice or ½ teaspoon of cloves or nutmeg to 1 cup of flour.

Delicious Feijoa Pudding

This really is a delicious pudding, crisp on top and pleasantly soggy at the bottom. It is quick and easy to make (and eat) and is equally good made with apples.

1 cup flour
1 teaspoon baking powder
25 g butter
milk or water
feijoas or apples
6-8 whole cloves
1 cup hot water
1 tablespoon butter
1 tablespoon sugar

Make a scone dough by sifting together the flour and baking powder into a bowl, rubbing in the butter and adding cold milk or water to mix. Roll the dough out flat and cover with peeled, sliced feijoas. Roll up the dough, put it in a buttered pie dish and stick the whole cloves along it in a row. Pour a cup of hot water over it in which 1 tablespoon each of butter and sugar have been dissolved. Bake about an hour at 180°C. Eat hot or cold.

Pear and Ginger Sponge

Fruit sponge puddings can be made from any peeled, sliced, fresh or stewed fruit and the spices can be varied to taste; for example, apples or plums and cinnamon or caraway, peaches and nutmeg, feijoas and cloves or whatever you like can be added. A little freshly grated lemon rind mixed with the fruit tastes good.

25 g butter
½ cup sugar
1 egg
1 cup flour
1 teaspoon baking powder
1 teaspoon ginger
½ cup milk
stewed or raw sliced pears

Cream the butter and sugar until light, add the beaten egg and mix well. Sift together the flour, baking powder and spice and stir in alternately with the milk to make a smooth batter. Half fill a buttered pie dish with sliced pears, pour the batter over and bake 1 hour at 180°C.

Blueberry Sponge Pudding

This blueberry pudding is nice to make for a change because the syrupy bottom contrasts with the drier sponge mixture, and when it is served with whipped cream it is a real treat.

1 tablespoon butter
½ cup brown sugar

2 cups blueberries
125 g butter
½ cup sugar
1 beaten egg
1 cup flour
1 teaspoon baking powder
milk

Melt the butter in a saucepan and stir in the sugar over a low heat. When it is all melted together add the blueberries, mix well and pour into a buttered dish. Cream the butter and sugar until smooth then add the beaten egg. Sift in the flour and baking powder and make into a batter by adding milk — about ¼ cup. Pour over the blueberries and bake 30 minutes at 180°C.

Grape and Ginger Ale Jelly

This is an American surprise! A moulded gelatine mixture of grapes, pineapple and citrus, flavoured with ginger ale that tastes tingly on the tongue. It is the sort of dish my aunts served on special occasions, and has the advantage of being able to be made several days in advance because it keeps well in the refrigerator. It is a true *pièce de résistance.*

2 tablespoons gelatine
4 tablespoons cold water
½ cup boiling fruit juice (e.g. apple, orange, pineapple)
½ cup sugar
½ cup ginger ale
juice of 1 lemon
250 g seedless white grapes
1 orange
1 grapefruit
2 kiwifruit
1-2 cups tinned pineapple
125 g crystallised ginger

Rhubarb crumble

Soften the gelatine in water for several minutes, then stir in boiling juice to dissolve it. Add the sugar, ginger ale and lemon juice and mix well. Leave until it begins to set. Then stir in the chilled, skinned and seeded grapes, sliced orange, segments of grapefruit, peeled, sliced kiwifruit and pineapple pieces. Chop the ginger finely and add it too. Pour into a wet mould and chill in the refrigerator until firmly set. To serve, place the mould briefly in a bowl of hot water to loosen the jelly. Put a large plate on top of the mould and turn it all upside down. Lift off the mould and garnish the jelly with fresh chopped fruit.

To peel grapes: pour boiling water over them in a bowl, just as you do to skin tomatoes and, when a skin will come off easily, pour the water away and skin them all. The skins come off easily when the grapes are properly ripe. Once they're skinned, halve the grapes and remove any pips with the point of a sharp knife.

Persimmon Ice-cream

The astringent persimmons which have a creamy texture when properly ripe may be eaten in the hand by removing the stem and scooping the centre out with a teaspoon, a bit like eating a boiled egg. They also make wonderful ice-cream.

2 cups persimmon pulp
1 cup sugar
juice of 1 lemon
1 cup whipped cream

Sieve the pulp and stir in the sugar and lemon juice. When well mixed fold in the whipped cream and freeze the mixture in a covered plastic container for about 2 hours so that it is still creamy and not full of ice crystals. Serve topped with chopped walnuts or slivered almonds.

NIBBLES

Tomato Tarts

Everyone loves pizza with its savoury tomato filling. These little tarts are savoury too but have a crisp pastry base, and thyme and sweet marjoram for seasoning. They may be served hot or cold and are an excellent lunch dish.

Pastry:
125 g flour
50 g butter
1 egg
pinch salt
iced water

Sieve the flour into a bowl and cut in the butter. Make a dough by adding the egg, salt and sufficient cold water, and kneading until it forms a smooth ball. Chill the dough for 30 minutes.

Filling:
1 onion
1 clove garlic
1 tablespoon safflower oil
500 g tomatoes
1–2 sprigs thyme
1 bay leaf
1 teaspoon sugar
salt and pepper to taste
1 teaspoon sweet marjoram

Cook the sliced onion and garlic gently in the oil for about 5 minutes until soft. Add the skinned, chopped tomatoes, thyme, bay leaf and sugar. Cook uncovered until thick. Season to taste with salt and pepper. Cool.

Roll out the dough and line patty tins or small pyrex dishes with it. Fill with the tomato mixture, sprinkle with chopped sweet marjoram. Bake at 200°C for 10–15 minutes until the pastry is crisp and light brown.

Rosemary Walnuts

Walnuts can be served sweet or savoury and this and the following recipe make tasty nibbles with drinks before dinner or with coffee afterwards.

1-2 tablespoons melted butter
1-2 tablespoons finely chopped rosemary
salt and pepper to taste
½ teaspoon cayenne pepper
1 cup walnuts

Melt the butter in a bowl, add the rosemary, salt, pepper and cayenne and mix well. Pour into a baking dish, add the walnuts and roll them in the mixture by shaking the dish back and forth. Bake for 15 minutes at 180°C, stirring every so often. When cooked, dry on waxed paper on a rack. Store in an airtight jar.

Spiced Walnuts

½ cup brown sugar
½ teaspoon salt
½ teaspoon cinnamon
1½ tablespoons water
½ teaspoon allspice
½ teaspoon nutmeg
2 cups walnuts

Combine all ingredients, except walnuts, in a saucepan and bring to the boil, stirring. Add the nuts, stir to coat evenly and tip out onto waxed paper to dry. Store in an airtight jar.

Nut Fudge

The trouble with home-made sweets is that they don't keep — they are so delicious they are eaten quickly.

This recipe is quick and reliable and comes from a fudge expert!

1¼ cups milk
3½ cups sugar
125 g butter
2 teaspoons vanilla essence
¼ cup sultanas
¼ cup blanched almonds or chopped walnuts

Heat the milk in a large saucepan, add the sugar and butter and stir until dissolved. Bring to the boil and boil 10-15 minutes until a small quantity of the mixture will form a tiny ball when dropped into cold water. Remove from the heat and stir in the vanilla, sultanas and nuts. Stand 5 minutes then beat the mixture with a wooden spoon until it is no longer glossy. Pour onto a lightly greased plate, smooth with a hot knife (dipped in hot water) and cut into pieces when cold.

Fresh Peach and Cheese Savoury

This requires ripe freestone peaches — not too big — and is still a dish that requires a fork rather than being a finger food. Watercress is the best accompaniment but landcress, rocket or lettuce will do.

cream cheese
chopped walnuts or almonds
chopped ginger
peaches
lemon juice

For each peach, roll a good teaspoon of cream cheese into a ball and roll this in chopped nuts and ginger. Peel and stone the peaches, put a cheese ball between two peach halves and press them together. Roll them in a little lemon juice and chill lightly before serving garnished with watercress and a little French dressing.

Rosemary walnuts.

Guava Jelly and Cheese

Serve a plate of water crackers with a dish of guava jelly and a cheese board containing gruyère and blue vein among others. Either spread biscuits with jelly and add cheese or spread biscuits with cheese and top with jelly.

Pear Savouries

My father was very fond of fruit with cheese and used to cut small chunks of cheddar to top pieces of apple and banana. I like cheese with pears too, and cream cheese and ginger and/or walnuts and almonds blend well with the texture of the fruit.

Delicious combinations follow, and you'll find many more if you experiment.

Pears with Cream Cheese, Ginger and Walnuts

crystallised ginger, finely sliced
fresh chunky chopped walnuts
cream cheese
pears

Combine ginger and walnuts to taste and blend into cream cheese with a fork. Use to fill the cavity of a halved cored pear and eat immediately. If you wish to prepare this early, brush the fruit with lemon juice to prevent it turning brown.

Pears and Blue Vein Cheese

Combine 1 part of blue vein cheese with 3 parts of cream cheese and serve with pears in the same way. A little paprika can be added and a dish of olives provided to accompany the pears.

Every man should eat, drink and enjoy the fruit of all labours; it is the gift of God.
    Ecclesiastes 111:13

Index